P9-BIY-635

JRNLS80s

FROM

SWANS

"Consciously extreme, physical music. Like standing in a room full of sledgehammers."
"...one moment of loss of memory, forgetting you're alive, losing consciousness."

NEW

SONIC·YOUTH

"Crashing bashing intensified dense rhythms juxtaposed with filmic mood pieces."
"evoking an atmosphere that could only be described as expressive fucked-up modernism. And so forth."

YORK

s.o.u.t.h.e.a.s.t
Sun · Nov 14 · CAT'S CRADLE · CHAPEL HILL, N.C.
Mon · Nov 15 · THE PIER · RALEIGH, N.C.
Tues · Nov 16 · THE 40 WATT CLUB · ATHENS, Ga.
Wed · Nov 17 · THE 688 CLUB · ATLANTA, Ga.
Fri · Nov 19 · THE 9:30 CLUB · WASHINGTON, D.C.
Sat · Nov 20 · THE MARBLE BAR · BALTIMORE, Md.

SONIC YOUTH - EP available on NEUTRAL records
SWANS - EP available on LABOR records

CBGB and OMFUG

315 Bowery (at Bleecker) (212)982-4052

24 HOUR PARKING AVAILABLE

Wed May 22
Filming for Japanese TV

THE RAUNCH HANDS
The Turbines • The Upstartz
The Buicks

Thurs May 23

THE PREVARICATORS
ED GEIN'S CAR
Next Generation • P.M.S.

Fri May 24

SONIC YOUTH
LIVE SKULL
Hope • Volcano Suns

Sat May 25

THE EGYPTIANS
Syntax Error
Verbal Drama
Figure Life Out

2:30PM Sat. May 25 HARDCORE MATINEE $5

THE F.U.'S
Malignant Tumor
No Milk On Tuesday

3:30PM Sun. May 26 HARDCORE MATINEE $5

Damage
Money Dogs
Bodies in Panic
Constraint

Sun May 26 Eve $7

TANK From England
A.O.D.

Mon May 27 - AUDITION SHOWCASE

Tues May 28
Brian Kelley • Beaujolais From France
Roo Ha Ha • Drone Sect

Wed May 29

IMPERIET

16 TRACK RECORDING AVAILABLE

JRNLS80s

Lee Ranaldo

*poems, lyrics, letters, observations, wordplay &
postcards from the early days of Sonic Youth*

Dedicated to: Amanda Linn and Cody Ranaldo; my Sonic co-horts: Kim Gordon, Thurston Moore, Steve Shelley, Bob Bert, Richard Edson and Jim Sclavunos; crew members Susanne Sasic, Terry Pearson, and John Erskine; David Linton and Truus De Groot, Carlos Van Hijfte, Stuart Somer, Jeff Cantor, Thom DeGesu, Rob Abramowitz, John Rogers, Mike Watt, David Klass, Danny Hamilton, Richard Brewster, Glenn Branca and Josh Baer, Barbara Ess, Rhys Chatham, Rudolph Grey, Arto Lindsay, Lydia Lunch, Burkhardt Seiler, Gerard Cosloy, Greg Ginn, Paul Smith, Pat and Liz Naylor, Edwin Pouncey, Epic Soundtracks, Catherine Bachman and Nicholas Ceresole, Richard Boone and family, many others absent here.

Thanks to Leah Singer for editing assistance and support.

Some of this material has been previously published, in slightly different form, in the following publications: *Killer, Forced Exposure, Road Movies, Big Hammer, Gonzo Circus, Crossing Border Magazine, Magic Mushroom, Verses That Hurt, Sonic Life* and *Coffeehouse.*

Published 1998 by Soft Skull Press
Edited by Sander Hicks & Karla Zounek
Cover design by Ryan McGinness
Book design by Susan Mitchell

©1998 by Lee Ranaldo
ISBN 1-887128-31-X
First Edition

"Dean took out other pictures. I realized these were all the snapshots which our children would look at someday with wonder, thinking their parents had lived smooth, well-ordered, stabilized-within-the-photo lives and got up in the morning to walk proudly on the sidewalks of life, never dreaming the raggedy madness and riot of our actual lives, our actual night, the hell of it, the senseless emptiness. pitiful forms of ignorance. 'Goodbye, goodbye.'"

—J. Kerouac

"I can't see anything.
All I can see is me.
That's all that's important
as far as I'm concerned.

My eyes can focus.
My brain is talking.
Looks pretty good to me.

Sometimes I talk to myself but I
really have nothing to say.
I could talk about going out
or having fun.

She thinks she's a goddess.
That she can talk to the spirits.
I wonder if she can talk to herself.
She don't know..."

—Eric Emerson
acid sequence from
Chelsea Girls

Mentholated Webs: 1980–1984

The dry heat of the radiators, the cold chill of the air coming through the windows. . . . People out on the streets, under the lights at this late hour, at all hours. Watching conversations in progress through the windows of the Odeon, the fancy downtown eatery—venetian blinds, ivory white, fragment my view of all the pretty people within. The lge. red neon sign overhead. The yellow glow of the street lamps. People hunched inwards, hands-a-pockets from the cold, eyeing each other w curiosity, w fear, w intent. Trucks roll even now, the city alive. The lights. World trades looming. The lights go off in unison, floor by floor extinguished beginning at 1 am, first in one tower, then the other. Automated efficiency. Automats. Yr food served outa time capsule; fresh; vacuum; *sanitaire.*

The click of red high heels on the pavement—another young couple out. The fancy dining rooms.

CLICK. CLICK. CLICK.

She holds his arm tight, like her pants. Designer pockets. His eyes—roving, moving, searching out the dark corners—dark black hair, a latin face—once a young tough.

CLICK. CLICK. CLICK.

The camera clicks, an arm goes up. The taxi, the opening door, the climb inside. Dark shapes in dark interior. Yellow Checker under yellow glow. His head turns once, around, and back. Destinations. The taxi pulls back into traffic.

CLICK. CLICK.

The frame freezes.

The frame freezes.

CLICK. CLICK. The shutter halts. That man on the bench with the too lge. jacket—it hasn't ever been washed—he freezes, hunched inside. Old shoes, old clothes, old dreams.

CLICK. CLICK. CLICK.

Old dreams are an endless commodity. A chain of events, a rent in the fabric of reality. A drain. Shoulders raw, spine twisted. Who knows how long they go on.

i) Who knows how long they go on? How many nights it takes

on a street bench, in a doorway, in old cardboard refrigerator boxes. How many nights does it take? How long are the cigarette butts tonight? How cold is it? How does the thirty-degree chill affect an empty stomach? Long empty eyes? Saturation points. Points in a stream that simply, suddenly, sometime, end.

ii) Who knows how long they go on? How long can such dreams go on? An endless ribbon of ideas, the light of tomorrow's day, turning a corner at full speed, legs aching, smack into the bricked up corridor. Back into the labyrinth. Time sense. Back into the frame. The shutter clicks.

He's picking through the NY City public garbage cans now—placed for your convenience.

"Sometimes they hold treasures, brother. Sometimes they sit knocked over, roll down windy West Broadway. *Sometimes* they even go right through the fancy glass storefronts."

Invade. Invoke. Enter the courtyard w the cypress trees. With the slate walkways, the manicured turf. The bushes w their dark waxy leaves. Colorful flowers line the paths. The statues. Turn to leave all this. The bricked up corridor. The darkening sky.

Rain on the park benches.

"They're not so comfortable when they're wet; other times they suit just fine."

So tell me of yr summer on the beach. The glare. The gradual incidence. The slopes' decline, the immaculate shore. Things you found there aren't worth a whole lot now. The sun dried up yr memories, good for you!, yr thoughts dried just like the sand dried onto yr back. Evaporated.

The glare hit you hard, yr eyes like ice against it, glassy mirrors. The trees were green. Then. Young couples sat under them in silence. Fingers ran through hair. Sleep comes in his lovers' arms. The embrace a cradle, a comfort, a seduction. Later seduction will be a threat. But later, not now in the shining sun. The glare from the water keeping eyes in close.

CLICK.

A scan of the shoreline.

CLICK.

Someone is running in the tall grass.
CLICK.
Someone has found something in the tall grass.
Someone is running in the glass.
Something is found in the glass.
CLICK. CLICK. CLICK.

Nov. 1980

---

when i'm dreaming
when i'm wide awake
when i'm freshly painted
when i'm dressed to kill
when i'm feeling natural
when i'm lost in thought
when i hit the ceiling
when nothing's going on
when i'm leaving
when i'm at home
when i hear you breathing
when i'm confused
when you see right through me
when i put you on
when your presence mattered

wait
to see what happens
wait
to be certain
just kill time
wait to be certain

when i'm on the right track

wait
to see what happens
wait
to be certain
just kill time
wait to be certain

november 1980
greene st. below broome, east side wall

---

tell me of
yr life
on the beach
this summer

the sloping incidence

the glare

11/20/80 monday
arnold's turtle

on a postcard to thom:

just after five o'clock, subdued afternoon atmosphere here at the restaurant. skies moving from grey to blue. a few people sit at tables, their hushed talk a warm glow in the chill. old men and women walk by these west village windows, bundled up in the face of winter's threat. pumpkins, leaves turning. the sun lighting the higher floors of the buildings, where roof tops do not block. a final flare before dusk, warm gold on white bricks. light, airy, yet enclosed like a cradle, like a womb. the shopkeepers still go about their business, although it is dusk, and yellow bulbs are being lit in bedrooms and kitchens. the autumn chill is giving me a warm feeling inside, and the city feels accommodating, feels good like a home. . . .

March 1981
in flight: Rome—A'dam

+ instruments

backwards glances
i'm tied up
divided lands
i'm crossing lines
political boundaries
i'm in love
two times
two times

looking through memories
i'm far away now

5

send them packing
i'm high up
looking in yr eyes
fills me up
i'm in love
two times
two times

looking at brown eyes:
i'm in love
looking into blue eyes:
I'm in love
packing up memories
shipping them home
i'm in love now
two times
two times

twice and falling
memory fading
changing my mind
two times
two times

26-7 july 1981

DESPAIR(ING)
[to Thom]

Well this day is finally coming to a close, the skies finally breaking, after promising
to all day, into a thunder and lightning farewell.

So I figure, nothing else having happened today, that I'll sit down, smoke another in what is becoming an interminable chain of cigarettes, and write.

I'm at a point of despair the magnitude of which I've known few times in my life. It is especially poignant right now, this last week in July as the summer doldrums set in, and everyone is afforded some avenue of escape, leaving town: David to France, Amanda to Chicago, *two* friends to Denver, I not among them.

I'm half tempted t hitch out to see you in a lost act of futility, twenty-four dollars in my pocket/to my name, readying to crack my head against the entire mass of this fucking planet. I am finding myself in a particularly hopeless mood—can't raise the energy to do anything, can't find the meaning in any aspect of my current life—just feel suddenly as if the bottom has dropped out from everything and I'm now a cartoon character suspended in mid-air, unknowing, about to find out the cliff has crumbled and plunge downwards after it. This world is just no fucking use. I can't unravel it. Can't find the motivation to do anything except read books full of other people's words. Can't find myself thinking one original thought, having one moment of insight or exaltation.

This basic downwards cast that has come over me—can't muster the energy to go out and look for some job I know I'll hate within days, even though I'm about as poor and busted as could be.

A job I'll hate, I can't muster for that. I don't know what's wrong. I've got friends here, feel somewhat at home here, if only I didn't feel this need for some sort of meaning I can't find or put into words, I think I'd be alright. But everything I encounter, every action, conversation or interlude, idea, problem, just seems so finite, so limited. I'm convinced for the moment that almost NOTHING anyone does can change *anything*, that we're all stuck in some great useless maze. What does it take to gain some sort of real satisfaction? I can find pleasure in the immersion in "self" that is an artists' lot, or in a zen-like bliss of just watching the world without participation. Or I can find fault with each in turn. Why must I be cursed with a mind that can see both of these? To place me smack in the middle of this dilemma.

I envy the ones who are stupid and mundane and desirous of nothing beyond their noses, no great redemptions or insights. I also envy the ones who manage to find inspiration and meaning without its resultant dark side: SELF DOUBT/BLACK TIDES.

I feel I just want to run and run and spend myself until there's nothing left and I just fold up somewhere and fade from this life. I know it's too easy a way out, but what is a person to do faced with these problems?

Sure I can make another drawing, write some verse, but what of it? It's not really going to change anything, and I'm under some sort of delusion that *actions should have effects*, should *mean something* larger than the finitude they seem to have. I can't stand the thought of a mundane life amidst desires for something bigger. Either I must erase these desires from my life/world, or find that cathartic grandeur I'm looking for.

What is it?
What is it?
I'm just not in a good way.
Where is it?

Here I am at the pinnacle of humanity, the product of thousands of years, I should be preparing to take the next step and I can't find my fucking shoes. *What the fuck is this goddammed problem?* Why is it so hard? This summer heat just blinds me, makes everything sweat with perspiration, makes any effort too much trouble.

The fires are burning dim. Can't figure out how to rekindle them. All seems lost and not even violent emotions will help now. There's no-one to turn to and no-one who really knows how to listen anymore. *If I can't do something for my own self then I just can't do anything at all.*

God, I haven't felt like this since those early years of college, when the future loomed unsure, before I'd come across something to sink into, some "art". Well now I've about re-emerged from that time. Mastered the early stages of something. It's been six years or so, and now I'm back at the question of how to put to use what I've learned—*craft is not enough;* now I must see what I can do with it. For me. It's the start of something new, a new climb up from the depths, maybe to greater heights than the last peaks, maybe to be swallowed up somewhere along the route. I just don't know, and now I'm pining over questions with no immediate answers.

I think I'm due to leave the city soon. I can feel it, Thom. I guess by next summer I may be gone. F. Scott Fitz, in *This Side of Paradise:* there's a line about "NY being an awful place to be unless yr on top." Right now I'm far from it and the heat of its furnaces may melt me down if I don't

GET
OUT.

Feel desperation.
That's all right now.
Ultimate, untimely despair.

Despair.

DESPAIR.

What the fuck is this all about?
I can't find it.
Can't find out.

CAN'T

CAN'T
CAN'T
do it
any
more

tonight.

And what kills me more than anything else, these damn street lights out my window still burn bright as hell, so efficient, as if nothing is *ever* the matter, *not a fucking thing is ever*

OF

matter out there, the world spins and doesn't take notice of any of it.

I'll go shooting off the deep end and it'll be just like some broken light bulb, a faulty bulb in a street lamp somewhere across the continent. They'll come along and replace it with a bright beauty and no-one will be any the wiser. Nothing, god-dammit, nothing will have

CHANGED,

NOTHING
WILL
BE
ANY
DIFFERENT.

Like a cloud that passes over the moon and then moves on to let the light shine again, I'll have come and gone, in a vision of despair, FAULTY CIRCUIT, and no-one will be any the wiser. And that is just what will be the shame of it all.

IT'S

THIS

VICIOUS

CHANGE

THAT

HURTS.

summer 1982

KILLED
HIS
WIFE,

THEN
SHOT
HIMSELF.

14 november 1982

first night out

first night out.
seventeen different propositions.
a point of light.
source.
bright glass on a chain being wound around us.
the relation ship.
the toiling of idle hands.
dipped in the stream.
dripping w guilt.
a secret form of punishment.
axes thru skulls.
shadow of futility.
endless/revolt.
the shifting of light and shadows.
dividing each existence.
no-one is right.
nothing is solid.

nothing can be held in one's hands
for long.
discontinuity.

nov 1982 Florence

---

twenty-five views of Florence, each one an individual study. no
two alike. take a trip through the winding cobbled streets, truly
as if being there. follow paths that lead straight into history:
the cracking plaster, the orange clay, the smell of coffee beans.

be sure of yrself.
take leaps down paths w no end in sight.
walk forwards.
never listen to anyone,
they'll always confuse you.
some people never learn.
some people never will.
you can't change yr fate.
you too can find unresolved desires to keep you going.
desires and demands to remain unsolved,
unsettling, *fucked*, for their lifespan.

3 june 1983 Sacred Sacre Bleu

Sacred sacre bleu. A vision of Glenn on the Sistine Ceiling. High above, in the vault with the young men, the prophets and sibyls. Body in motion, twisting in sculptured space. A sculpting in the air, slowly, hovering. Revolving in a mad rush, slow motion filmed. Silently turning, the sound so loud it becomes the silence. Two as one. Thousands of voices cry out at once. And are one.

But Glenn on the Sistine Ceiling remains. Possessed. Immortal. Mute, poised for eternity, about to issue an endless cry, any century now, to shatter the silence and crash down on the patterned tiles below.

3 june 1983
before paris (which would change everything)

Traveling in France Now

Travelling in France now, going to Paris, and on to Poitiers. I've never been to France before—this is the first time. So far: great. The feel here is different, older. Sedate.

I like the small towns. Brick bldgs, worn years. Nasal voices and stupid sentiment. The gendarmes come and I make some fun w the language. Screaming *"Pourquoi pas?"* (why not?) at them. Speaking a blistering fumbleFrench and the frogs just look on and speak back in cultured Englais. Nuclear plants alongside the ancient stones along the train route. Atomic sonnets. It's brilliant w golden sun. Summer has been w us since England and Amsterdam. Brilliant sun gilt on the lush green. Thurston is screaming into the wlkmn microphone. The girls, Barb, Amanda, Arleen and Margaret, look at him strange. But as I said the sun has gilt the lush leaves, the red clay roofs and orderly garden plots. The ancient stone steps. Red brick window frames. Thurston laughing at the sounds.

Clouds hang high, hover in *bleu* above the stretching scape of green and gold. Lazy nasal voices, I come to a woman, skirted in the golden field. *Blauer Augen.* I scream scream scream till sore. The noise is incredible, a violent din. A blazing spirit-wall, noise like a spectre rushed over the landscape. Passing between the tall thin trees, skirting the streams and canals, where boats slowly lull fr side to side. Still looking at me, she now silent. Wondering. I stare, 'midst this field. I point her to the graveyard, old stones in splendor. Small walled courtyard. Hungry, still; stiff w ancient life. The gravestone crosses slowly fading, turning to earth, into the earth, banging together and breaking in a flash of light, the ultimate religion. I walk w her, together we, through this manicured landscape. Pristine crystal, polished mirror facets. Where Cezanne and Monet walked. I walk w her, I can see her soft flesh, rounded smooth shoulders. She runs now, not pretty but w a fear bred from this rushing wind.

I surface: above the blue I can see the land clearly now. Clear head. Clear mental head. Metal head. Steel blue. I can move w certainty. All that I had thought, all the confusion of being, of eyes seeking, is now subsumed. A tent on the horizon. Never reached. Left unoccupied. On the gilded plain, edge of this world.

Alone and running I find all the rock walls crumbled. No more dark places. No more dark fears, this sunlight, this freedom. I feel both. I am both. The hurried walk no more. The girls wait. I watch. No need speech. All are watching. Some from the little round windows, high up in ashen bldgs. Sunlight streaming, sacred, scarring their vision. They look to the horizon, the gilded green plain still, as though bronzed, each leaf a heavy weight, nothing moving on the earth, the wind a hollow whistle thru this static scape. No one is talking and that's just as well. For no one need ever talk. The end came. Golden. France in silent movies waits. . . .

Sadie

One of those fucking awful black days where nothing is pleasing and every thing that happens is an excuse for anger. An outlet for emotions stockpiled. An arsenal. An armor. These are the days when i hate the world. Hate the rich, hate the happy, hate the complacent—the TV watchers, beer drinkers, the satisfied ones. Because i know i can be all those little hateful things, and then i hate myself for realizing that. There is no preventative directive or safe approach to living. We each know our own fate. We know from our youth how we are treated, how we are received, how we shall end. These things don't change. You can change yr clothes, or hair, friends, cities, continents, but sooner or later yr own self will always catch up, always it waits in the wings.

Not happy with yrself? Better get used to it cause it ain't going away, maybe duck out for awhile, but not too long. Always returns. Angry. Fucking. Spirit.

If you're reading this let me tell you those words have been spit: Ang-gry. Fuck-king. Murderous Spirit. Damnable youth. murderous youth shit-kicking and spouting spiritual. Sonic fuckking youth. Fountains.
Dont give a damn.

Dont give a damn.
about you and yr youth.
change yr clothes and dress for rape, or success.
camouflage yr feelings in a satin red dress.
put me up or put me out but you try to suck me in.
I wont give you that pleasure again.
Keep yr uniform on so yr friends will know who you are. Then
crack open in front of them.
Crack yr skull.
Pressure on yr/my skull.
Unfocus yr eyes if you can.
That's the only good thing I've learned.

The you is me here.
So fuck me.

24 november 1983
groningen

Visiting Smithson's Broken Circle/Spiral Hill

The blood is coursing through me and I feel its rush. Three AM flat in Holland night. We drove across the barren *plein* this afternoon, empty fields straight lines of trees, hogs and cows not raining but cloudy and w Dutch mist hanging lightly everywhere.

We went to Emmen on the way to see Smithson's Broken Circle/Spiral Hill, on my insistence, everyone either half-hearted or against it. Not able to see the beauty of a wild goose chase through the flatlands.

By the time we reached Emmen, night had fallen, but still we pressed onwards. Too late to turn back. We were told it was down a dirt road and "not to get our hopes up" because it was in a very deteriorated state. Drove the whole bumping length of the road in the just darkling night and came to the end w o finding anything.

Drove back along, slower. Found just a no parking sign, then I spot a rise of earth through the trees, which of course stands out a bit here in sea-level-land. We see there is a small break in the fence w signs saying No Trespass, and No Dogs and No Swimming; BUNCHA NOES. We figure this must be it.

A break in the fence, a dirt path and yes, feeling our way through darkness, moon under cloud cover so there is little light, vision a haze which clouds the darkness, can see merely basic shapes, color contrasts. But it is Broken Circle/Spiral Hill. We ginger down the path to it, through underbrush which has grown, is growing, over it, reclaiming the place in a way RS would surely; have loved. The hill is now a rough mound, its clean lines long gone, shrubs growing on its sides, and grass, it was a large sad heap, not really sad but no longer w new shoes, shall we say.

The circle was also fading, the water inlet still seemingly intact for the most part, the large central boulder still holding, claiming its ground. The jetty was completely submerged, back to the quarry-sea, like The Spiral Jetty. Wether it hovered inches below the surface we could not tell in the darkness.

So we came and saw, or rather felt the deteriorating beauty, the end of everything, return, return, return, we speak of truths that deteriorate naturally over time. Worn out by the sun and moon, the tides. Time stands still we know, and yet time is all surrounding, a misty beaming stream in which we grope.

The changes that come about are as if from thin air. We want, we love and hate, we gnash our teeth on stones, unwilling to yield. It's unclear if we can yield, destroy the surface tension of the sea. So we feel and are lifted. Armed and dropped, dragged under. Cool blue. Under cover. We believe. We reach. We grab and run.

When we assume, we are lost, we know nothing really, and only a bit first hand, but we assume so much. Take anyone's word for anything. We like the sound of words, they befriend us and slop into our pockets only later to crawl up and out, slithering up into our throats to clamp down. The pleasure of death, "Why thank you". Have another cigarette and see death jump.

1983

---

keep me alive
fragments of a life once lived
wash me away
ask me for an answer
come rip the mask
come tear the seat
cum sweetly in bed
drift off and then wait
find yrself waiting for a moment
waiting for time to look
BACK

CLEAR HAZE
you are here : : :YOU ARE THERE

travelling through this grey landscape brings back the feelings and thoughts of varied, distant pasts. why does the roadway, cruising the hiway ribbon in a little bubble, always evoke these past tenses? linear time evocation. the lakes and ponds lay like spatial sinks, indicating no particular time or depth. throwing back onto the sky its own reflection, dull grey-green.

The heat has settled over the land, the air breaks up into coarse granules which rise and fall, swirl and eddy. My reasoning is pushed into some far-flung corner of this atmosphere. I move along, slicing thru the air, slightly faster that it, body motions ahead of conscious thought. Where thought comes in waves, physical movement is a constant.

a deep dullness takes hold of me way out here on these backwater american plains. solitary old bldgs, and empty lots full of discarded debris stand frozen in time, sealed in the solid atmosphere of time-space. a place that is everywhere and nowhere at once. a point on a line. a dot on the plains. corridor tunnel of sinking asphalt. *green chute, bellyup.* arms extending to infinity (which begins at the edge of town).

6 june 1984

Saw a group body popping and breaking on the sidewalk at Sheridan square today, by Crazy Eddies. Popping up on cardboard for the crowd.
The crowned kings.

EMPATHIC REACTION.
Real cool.

With greased palms, slate idols slip and glide. singing across the cardboard sea.

25 june 1984

something about this day

something about this day. fear and evil running helter-style, close to the surface. an about to open wound. just now on the IRT a black/white racial slurring contest of pure and vicious hatred. any excuse for explosive violence will do. before that our radio show gig for timmy sommers—on the way our cabbie is charged and chased by a Hell's Angel down fifth street. FOR BLOWING HIS HORN! the angel was out for blood. and our cabbie pulls his blade without batting an eye. long rusty blade, he's waving it in a circle out the window and screaming insults back at the guy chasing us. the cab is pelted from the stoops by sitting toughs. i told him we were late for the show, w no time for a murder. it's on their minds. . . . we got away, i guess. and then just now young suburban type kids doing "Heart of Gold" and other 60's folk-rock songs (twenty years!) which should be left to live in dignity in the dusky past instead of being paraded on sheridan square for the doped middle class to gawk at from their cars. *where are those kids?*

July 1984
Clem

Someone dreams, something's burning. Images abound. The music stops and the silence is unending. The outside is forever closing in. Falling forwards in the city of tension. Eyes cross, eyes meet, eyes part and cast deliberate shadows. Across a jet trail in the sky. Across the river that runs the length of the city. Across the empty dawn. Eternity, rising.

This is the day that lasts forever. This is the time that will not stop. These are the years going nowhere. Waiting to drop. Waiting to soar and release. Waiting for a moment of conclusion.

Someone is breaking glass out on a street. Sending scattering shattered shards of light out across the asphalt. Like signal flares, dimly glowing in a dark cavity.

Somewhere right between yr eyes
I found a well
I step in and I'm falling
Deep down a dark damp drain
I can't help myself
Your wish is my demand
I am nothing if not you
I am you
YOU KNOW ME
Command me
I'll do anything
for you
I'd even kill
for you
And I would die
for you
do anything
to be you.

january 1985
L.A.

other images, LA '85:

the city lit up, seen
at night from a distance,
glimmering wet,
twinkling and glistening,
lizard like thru the
haze of heat and debris,
struggling to crawl along
the contour of the earth.
constantly shifting,
unchartable

the complex freeway
over and underpasses

the sculptured
manicured trees

the desert
at night, expanse
full moon bright in
a wild ring
thru the haze

a new city in a new year

this is the end of our first full day here in LA tomorrow is the gig out in the mojave desert, 100 miles from here. already i've seen and felt more of LA than in previous trips. kim's folks have a classic california home, w clay-pot roof and beaut. spanish style window-frames, elegant and unlike the New England clapboard style which i know so well. we have cruised up sunset strip and on the freeways and blvds., we went to the shopping mall and also spent some time in an underground parking garage, which seems to be a classic part of this scene. we drove by the film studios, had burritos, went up in the hollywood hills. everything is clean and wide, spread out. green everywhere, carefully manicured and w shaped shrubs on every lawn, every hill. we visited all the wavoid shops on melrose—all of which amount to nothing. buncha junk. the blue skies go on endlessly in every direction.

tonite we made the Anti-Club scene to see the Meat Puppets, who as usual were great and weird. they strike me different every time i see them. local "knowns" were there. something about this place is very enticing, clean and healthy, wide open and fresh air in spite of common knowledge of temperature inversions, killer smog and quake-fear. yet my initial few hours of infatuation have been tempered by some sense that this is all facade, that something very banal or very sinister lurks beneath the trimmed hedges and pastel colored stucco. but at this moment the constant sunshine (i'm here twenty-four hours and already i'm certain it's always out there) and beautiful warm skies have me suckered in.

6 jan 85

words spoken in the desert
voices drifting across an open plain

tonight four walls move closer
tonight four walls close in

i stood last night out on the open plains and i heard voices moving towards me, burning red holes in the ground, leaving glowing embers of language as their gift. i was alone out on the desert plain under a dark sky-in-motion, full moon circled in a ring of voices, chanting silently, moving in and out. i was alone w a set of eyes which bore into mine. i know those eyes. "i know you," i said, and would explain no further. eyes blinking, pressing me, reflecting red from the fires. i took some several steps but felt no real warmth. an offering of mystery w o boundaries. i could not speak. there was no way to touch. the skin falls away from my hands. beautiful corridor of sight—we met in the air. soft. red. warm. deep dark. opaque. thoughts moving on the winds. emotions become a tangible atmosphere. a cool breeze, charged w current and ready to bristle and glow. rings of light.

after awhile it all stopped and i was standing cold in the aching sands. no wind; no nothing moving. no animals. a green glowing ring around the moon hangs. hills encircle us far off in every direction, giant basin of sand and brush.

was it to be shrugged off?
time will tell.
it was time to start the engines and move out.

jan 21, 1 AM
from seattle, 35,000' over washington state

the tour is over. we took off from sea-tac airport just an hour ago, en route to st. louis and then on to NYC. the clearest night for flying i could imagine. we lifted slowly and gradually made one long circle around seattle, climbing. the familiar shapes of land and water massed. snaking chains of streets and freeways, came into view. the higher we rose the clearer everything became, w no loss of definition. the lights twinkling everywhere, and the stars overhead as well, hanging, sus-pended over the curve of the earth. as we slowly rolled thru the air, lights blinked off and on in a flurry thru the blackness, moving in and out of the foliage below. finally some wisps of clouds began to blur the image, although for a long time i could still see the lights of boats on puget sound, and the circular ring of lights around the kingdome. then the blackness of uninhabited landscape took over.

i sense this ending, w vague melancholy and regret—that familiar sense of losing something that had been held in the hand. the closing of a door to a world one had inhabited for a period of time. keller told me that the original translation of the word sojourn is not journey but rather something closer to brief habitation in a place. closing the door on another sojourn. not that anything in particular is lost, it's just that sense of emptiness—leaving behind people, places, conversations, certain eyes . . . shops and stories, memorable times . . . moving towards a future which, familiar as it might be, is still an unknown quantity.

moving on thru the black night. we always seen to be moving on—leaving things behind. it's interesting, i like the idea of being on this side of the line. we make quick friendships w people who want to know us, are willing to help us out. folks who will put us up and take us around. be infused w our spirit and our sometimes raucous roller-coaster style of living. we afford them a glimpse of something that seems like freedom, and then move on again, somewhere else. i guess it has its empty spots as a lifestyle, but the communication w so many people is good, how-ever fleeting. both onstage and thru conversations i feel that we have a power to help open people's eyes, and minds, even if just a small bit. we try and get folks to see things differently. and it's not, thankfully, that we are holding a specific moral stance as much as that we are trying to say that people who want, and try, can succeed. people w sane morals and desires, complicated certainly, but not totally messed up w the insane blackness at the heart of so much current society. we're really pretty sane people, i guess, as down to earth as possible inside of such a weird vocation.

how nice it has been also to be out of NYC for a time. it's a fact that none of this would be real or possible without the city as a base to operate from. i feed off it as a place to live and i love its energy, have learned to accept living there. but it sure is a pleasure to leave and to float thru real landscapes w gorgeous trees—i was so impressed by the many great looking and different trees out here on the west coast. how weird for such a mundane item as a tree to make such an impression! to hang in a real house like kim's parents' great house in west LA or the place we just left in seattle where julie whitney is staying. a real house would be wonderful, although they are singularly sedentary things. wonderful for the permanence of closets and basements and backyards. yet i see a house as embodying a destruction of sorts. it becomes a determining force in your life. you no longer move freely about. people become so devoted to their houses. strange.

maybe one of the things i like about travelling, and all the people you meet is that one doesn't get tied into relationships that try to last for ages. Really close friendships w real communication are so rare that they almost seem impossible. but fleeting friendships—brief exchanges of ideas and info—talking w new people seems very real. you can usually only take things so far with people before everything meaningful is said, so it's nice somehow to meet so many new people w whom to exchange ideas. that old concept of the great morass, of an ever widening circle of friends and communication. i like the idea. meeting new faces free from the chains of longevity.

ideas flowing across years. . . .

16 mar
NYC

about 1 am, just returned from rosinante's pub where we all met after lydia's performance. where roli got thrown out in what was nearly a drunken brawl; he got too excited and germanicly drunk, wanted to crack a bottle over lyle's head just to hear the sound of it! they had to come and drag him away, the whole bar watching, bartender in his white apron and roli really wild and screaming "wimps! you're all wimps!" or "rrrimps!" w his accent. he was half putting on and half serious, at once drunk out of his mind and stone cold sober, completely and totally himself. they threw him out and thom almost got into the fray w some guy looked like kenny rogers who seemed just to be waiting for a chance to jump in. it was an exciting moment. we were brought alive and all focused for a moment on what was happening to this one person. roli let himself go, didn't give a shit for propriety or self-picture or *anything*—he wailed with the moment. so as sorry as it was in one way, in another it was a liberation, which is always grand; it was a shedding of veils and an exposé of what lies lurking. bravo! everyone came to attention around him.

Europe 1985
brown notebook journals

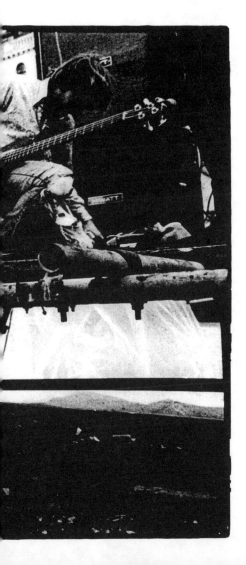

and now i sit here waiting. a video monitor for my head. electrons racing thru my mind. we've been here some three days now—it's quite cold and grey, the same old rock scene stuff is going down here as anywhere, only the haircuts have been changed to protect the innocent. fashion and class consciousness are so acute that when you meet someone relatively removed from it it's a surprise. they seem so "un-english."

all the kids are trying hard to be the next big one, w o really knowing what it will mean if they make it— besides a release from their immediate, dull lives. how long can the double life of a person in public view go on?

the climate here strikes me so oppressively this time through. cold wet and damp so much of the year, no real efficient heating. everyone seems used to the lack of warmth, but i see its effects. pasty faces, pale and either lined or jowled w those english jowls—people here often seem much older than their years. the body gets used to a less hospitable climate, but it does seem to age faster. it certainly allows you to tell the working class from the upper classes. why should such observations mean anything? why should such thoughts arise? it beats me.

paul says we can be "the next birthday party" if we want. what would that mean? could we handle it, do we want that possibility? it would be good to reach more people. no matters of lasting value need enter in that regard.

i feel quite dull now—cold and tired. jet lagging rather than ill i suppose. i hope. i don't know what tonight's show will bring. we saw the queen mother in her car today. it seems that's a big deal.

---

on broken circle/spiral hill and robt smithson

Quiet
quiet now
don'tsayaword

> square
> supplants
> circle
> the will to logic
> the will to love

BROKEN CIRCLE, SPIRAL HILL
went to emmen today, way home from groningen in holland north, dragged them all down the same dirt road to see it again. it was so fast i barely remember it. the sky was clouded over, just after the rain, a nice pale blanket. the water was a lovely green as though mixed with white. such an odd color. the day clearing up (from rain) just before we arrived—i took it as a sign of something. anyway, i saw it. climbed through the gate which read (i think, in dutch) "keep out" —i don't know why— climbed through and under the barbed wire into the adjacent cow pasture, for a better photo view. the circle has been greatly restored since last year, but it didnt look at all like photos i had seen of it— which is cool, i can (can't) imagine what the last supper looked like to leonardo— what we see is a grand permutation of an image. image becoming ikon. image becoming idea, nothing one really sees.

*   *   *

what else about the smithson piece? in the sleepy ville of emmen, which seems to maintain the piece in one breath, and to be unaware of its existence in the next. on our first visit in november 83 no one seemed to know of it at all. we ultimately discovered the location from a petrol station attendant. we had to drive down a very worn road, unpaved, to get there. it was dark by the time we finally found it, unmarked except for a dutch version of "no trespassing." we could barely make it out, certainly we couldn't see the shoreline, or the bare trees in the distance, or even the general shape of the surrounding quarry.

at that time, even in the darkling light it was apparent that the piece had fallen into a vast entropic well. the spiral hill was an undefined mass of overgrowth. as for the "circle," the land bridge was submerged and the canal had collapsed and filled in with earth. all that remained unchanged was the central boulder, and that, which smithson had disliked to begin with, has become the single most immutable facet of the piece. maybe that's the very reason he disliked it—its central focus and its resistance to erosion, to time. but i suppose at some point it too will shudder and tumble into the quarry lake.

this year in contrast the piece was restored, everything back to some approximation of the original relationship. like a folk song it is rebuilt w slight alterations, the spirit remaining more important that specific boundaries. we saw it in wonderful cool diffused light— rich pale greens and blue-greys.

this piece reminds me of his PARTIALLY BURIED WOODSHED in many ways . . . . it seems closer to that piece somehow than to the mirage of SPIRAL JETTY, which existed in its perfect state and then was suddenly gone, as though a figment. like the artist himself the Jetty went from full flower into memory, no intermediate stages, no slow fade of the kind built into the WOODSHED piece, or that which has taken place with BC/SH.

i felt greatly privileged to see the piece. i had to drag the same carload of disgruntled folks that came there one and a half years ago—no-one could understand my need to return to see it again. perhaps the most important artist of the century, he himself might not have understood the need to see this "crystal out of time."

he lives on as a memory, his work carried forth mostly in terms of abstract thought or the museum pieces. how many who have seen and liked one of his "non-sites" have actually been spurred on to visit the original place? is this an important consideration? somehow even in the "flesh" the exhibited pieces seem abstractions, while a visit to BC/SH is something of another sort altogether. a spiritual reunion. a confirmation of things known and unknown.

on the way out in the car K. asked what was the intent of this piece; i didn't quite know how to answer this question simply. the answer is for me bound up in everything i feel smithson was and stood for, strived for, plus my own vision of his vision on top of that. i felt that the visit to the site was so important, the main focus of my involvement with the piece right now. to replace the image from some catalogue repro with the experience of the real thing. that was my immediate goal. the cult of experience, unquestioning. reproductions, useful reference tools possibly, are an abhorrent substitute for the art itself. let's not reduce the spirit of art to one of cataloguing images for a slide show or yet another article.

i want to stand in front of the physical work and decide for myself. if painting loses that, it has lost everything. those who would rather read texts w repros that look at the real and decide for themselves have long ago missed the point. to see it in the real landscape of a backwoods abandoned dutch quarry, in emmen, merely a small dot on the map of holland, nowhere incarnate from the viewpt of 57th st., 2000+ miles away, in another universe. i could offer no verbal abstractions that held up in the light of simply being there, standing on that grassy hillside looking out and down at it. it became a "place" at last, no longer a notion. that was enough.

someone else in the car cynically remarked that they didnt see very much, and jokingly or sarcastically queried where was smithson now, where did this get him? (admittedly it was my folly, my trip, i had dragged them all along). all i could think to answer as we jolted our way back up the wet and crusty road was that it had "gotten" him everything, and that he was right back there, behind us, passing through a rusty gate portal and out into the open landscape.

7 apr 85

arriving in roma in ten minutes, eighteen hours on the train. i'm numb from the ride, slept all through the gorgeous golden light of tuscany, slept all night thru the darkling italian alps and southern france.

the whole thing began in a seedy bruxelles train station, all manner of characters on the loose and wandering the claustrophobic corridors in a low-ceiling'd belgian haze.

all the familiar italian faces come back to me, i see my past again, it's a bit easier to be objective this time. when was i here last? 1981 w glenn, and then for thirty-six insane hours of stalking the cold late night streets demanding money, threatening insanity and carnage to bewildered romans, and a late last minute plane outta here.

the sun has just slipped behind the massing clouds, on its way out of the picture. what style this city has. everything on an even keel, not too fast, people take their time and seem to know how to enjoy each other's company. the grandeur of the past is not held over the present, this city goes on in its own way, as vital now as it was then, eternal.

10 april 85
roma—firenze—zurich

sitting in the aisle now, jammed full super charged <<treno>> en route to zurich, packed full w all sorts of smoky bread-eating wine-drinking italians, and german school kids, all going back to life after the easter holidays. this giddy mood i feel is actually one of utmost desperation—laughing to keep from crying. we're stuck in the aisle, in the smoking seats, being racked back and forth by the rails. we may be here all night. it's a long ride and as soon as we get in to zurich tomorrow we've got to jump in a van and drive for eight hours in order to freak out some crowd of nameless, faceless austrians.

so the tour begins again, and roma fades slowly to the south. we were all over the city last night, out late w maria and steve eating marvelous food in some small trattoria in *tras tevere,* the region across the river, near the chieza de sta. maria.

as the beer and wine went down with the pasta things began to slowly explode around us. some girl at the next table w two guys, all very drunk, told steve she thought he was cute—quite improper—which initiated a twisted and involved exchange between maria and one of the guys, and between the girl (in french and italian) and bob (in english). in short, within minutes everyone was screaming with romantic fervor in that very italianate manner, the waiter and other patrons all jumping into the fray. me shouting "we're all drunk!" in pidgin italian, maria arguing endlessly w one of the guys. for sport. the waiter laughing, nodding agreement that he too was drunk (and looked it, although a fine upstanding gent/perfect italian waiter/signor.

that was the beginning of a long night out walking through the city, over to the great *piazza campidolio,* designed by buonarotti, along the forum-way, and to *piazza venezia* w its million-stepped, eternally flaming tomb of the unknown soldier.

the bus home took forever to come, and on it we listened as the bus-man argued w some young italian "punk" whom we deduced was making out in public w his hot-pink-haired girl friend on his lap, and maybe getting just a bit too into it for the conductor's liking. another heated italian exchange, w the same beautiful voices rising and falling, in heated argument of the kind where no-one seems to care about the outcome. it's more a means of interaction w each other, i think. they love it.

on the way home we ran into a funny bum and later set a car alarm screaming when i bumped my knee into the fender. incredible.

switzerland came up with the dawn today, rising high under hanging grey clouds, to white peaks. the air cool after the warmth of italia. it was a bleary morning for me, having spent an abysmal night on the overcrowded train, packed full to bursting. spent some time trying to sleep in the overhead luggage rack in the aisle, but nothing seemed to work. finally thurston and i managed to squeeze into a compartment w a family of germans, i believe, but who seemed to lapse back and forth between german and italian speech. very interesting, especially the two kids, playing cards, who in one round began counting "eins, zwei. . ." and in the next "uno, due. . . ."

switzerland is beautiful, more hauntingly majestic that i remember it—each country has such a specific feel this time. the landscape divides this continent into natural borders; each has its own feel from the first glimpse. i'd forgotten how individual they were, or maybe it never struck me before.

right now the sun is streaming, morning-bright. we ride along the *Zurichsee*, a beautiful slate blue through the tudor towns and respectable upright swiss villages. travelling is such a specific state of mind—my viewpt mainly takes the form of observations—"things look so"—much more than the deeper introspection i find i fall into at home. here, the world is presenting itself daily, straightforwardly, and there is too much too close to really question—too much to do for that to happen now.

12 april 85
dornbirn, austria

BLIND FANTASY #2

dark stage
drum kit either side

drummer one led out, blindfolded w long black sash, led to kit, to sit. drummer two led out, blindfolded same, to sit. they wait.

after a time, one starts up, snare beating. the other joins. they play only snare at first, somewhat organized and together. eventually it breaks down and they are each just *WAILING* away, no concern for each other. *out of synch*.

i am led out, blindfolded same, to center mike. to verbalize awhile across the din. psychedelic lights flashing. after awhile i turn for gtr to be handed. WAIL w in the din. quit, turn am led away. drummers are shoulder tapped, and led away also.

ENDE.

13 april 85
dornbirn, austria

Alpine Traum

that wonderful purple that hangs under the eaves at twilight, and washes cool thru evening trees. the color of nighttime sunshine, an indigo flame, bathing dark nights in desire. wrap me in those depths. i breathe in the cool blue where money floats but doesn't talk, in a chain of unbroken thoughts. cars hiss by my window, yet nothing is revealed. i am secreted away in dark depths. a dream, in purple shades, with a lover, by an opaque sea. an eternity. an obsidian sky. one frozen moment, fixed forever.

these cliffs go on forever and of course they never move, never falter. they stand at the gates of the world. this vision in blues and greens is an everlasting one. it might be said that i will never leave this place — land of the child-spirits! we move up the side of the world. far off some village lies, and glints welcome, brilliant beneath penetrating beams, at the base of the dark cliffs, below the deep green earth of the slopes.

a young genius walks the streets there. the pressure of ten thousand acres of hard rock upon his skull, waiting to explode, with thoughts winding in and out and over the course of the land like the rows of the terrace'd vineyards. his lover lies out in the landscape, arched, longing, far across the lake, below the snowfields. christine.

through the regular order of the rows, the streets and houses, the gleaming light of the boy's shining mind runs threads. he weaves a network of internal logic that eventually blankets the town. his own vision snaking its way up and out over the surface of this intuitive carpet. everything is known (to him). all the forms exist (for him). from the first moment, the first movement, nothing is left hidden, and yet nothing revealed. he grins. with a slow wrinkle of his forehead the logic carpet is lifted, shaken,and unfurled again. this time lying in a new configuration across the land. rising up he walks across the beads of light casting shadows which scorch and lay clear all things–eternity is revealed in one aspect after another. vision is incomplete, every viewpt. in his head is one of many. every vision is fiction, every dream fact. faster, faster now the images in his mind shatter into a thousand synthetic shards, the world a cubist visage for a moment, and then, the logic cape shook once more, gone, all gone, his lover waiting in the fields.

15 apr 85
switzerland

somehow the road is a sweet comfort, and everything seems fine and manageable as long as there's a white line beating time at sixty miles per. now, up in the suisse mts of *Vaudoise*, amongst the clouds, i feel quite alright. dropping off on the right are terraced fields and towns built right into the mtnside. below the lake of Geneve (lac Leman to the suisse) is an expanding plane, absolutely still, opaque w no surface reflection. a dull liquid cloud laid flat like a sheet. far across are towns that look as though they lie right at the base of the mtns.,as though out in the backyards there would be a vertical wall of rock.

the mountains go on forever and of course they never move, never falter. they stand at the gates of the world. this vision in blues and greens is an everlasting one.

it might be that tomorrow this view will only be a memory for me. its place taken perhaps by the canyons of cement and steel, or some other dream. it might also be said that i will never leave this place. . . .

april 21, 85
eindhoven

we saw:
  how the continents are fading
  how the elevator goes up
  the sound kettle
  the mirror room
  the infinite scale
  atomic time—one sec in 30,000 years

the first images of man, in stone
hydro-carbon chains
thomas edison, in palms
the groove
the living things
color spectra
no universals of any kind
an overload of the mind
weightlessness
3-d tv
a brief glimpse of god
towers to the sun
stonehenge in floral wreaths
the shape of sound

21 april, 85
eindhoven

---

postcard to thom

once more, man, from holland. we're back here for two days of rest before on to final u.k. blowout. as always on tour, my head is now filled w 1,000,000 ideas for my return—it's always that way—the travel is to grow <<*rapide*>>—to see—and home time is to assimilate ideas. right now my list of thoughts is many kilometers long—hafta tella bout it.

25 april 1985
u.k.

travelling now thru the lush hilly regions of north central england, en route to manchester. dense moss-covered woodlands, cold and wet, completely overhung w clouds. an occasional glint of sun, beaming down rembrandt-esque out of the dim light. red brick working-class towns, damp the year round inside and out. the folk damp themselves w ale to ward it off, to shut it out.

it feels like i've seen about half the world from the windows of a coach or train. i'm wondering what good it is. i suppose i'm seeing all there is to see—the cities and the way people talk, the look of their buildings, the lay of their land and the look in their eyes.

are these people aware of their obsessions, their repressed desires? do they know about the torn seam in the reality envelope? they move diligently forward, gratefully blind to light that will not warm them.

even the architecture in england seems so sorrowful and pedestrian, tedious. something which is merely better than nothing. world war depression architecture. we're in manchester now. we're here.

27 apr 85
stonehenge

on the way back to london now, returning from salisbury plain, from stonehenge. what a day—by the time we hit the plain a harsh, blustery morning had turned beautiful, a cold but jewel-like sunny day. shafts of light, right out of constable, pat said, breaking thru the clouds. what beautiful countryside. england earns the description "lush." stonehenge was smaller than we'd pictured, surrounded (since '78) by barbed wire and protected by little rope railings to keep folks out of the central ring. on the basis of our needing a photo for the next lp we were granted permission to forego the ropes and enter the circle. this came right as we were about to give up hope and go—i approached the guards, who turned out to be good old blokes—had sat guard on the 'henge for twenty-odd years, told us stories and lewd jokes. they were there in '65 when the beatles were filming *HELP!* across the plain.

the difference between viewing the thing from around, and then from within, was quite marked. from the outside it seemed like a sequence of still images, as though looking at a processed memory. it was not a thing felt. but from within the circle the stones revealed some bit of their powers, their texture. lichens clinging to rocks moved into position 4000 years ago. the sightlines began to make sense—you could view thru the plinths and out over the marker stone w the lizard head cut in, to where the solstice sun would rise. the whole thing took on a more majestic beauty, it took on reality, even across the span of years and in spite of the tourists and the wire fence, etc. we didn't see the makers, long dead, not even druids hanging around but we could certainly feel that this place held something— the architectural achievements of our ancestors. now it actually belongs to those two wardens, and the dozens of cows grazing in the fields just past it, they live w it and it's not a tourist attraction to them, or an album cover shot. to them its an actual part of reality.

i was thinking about the ground covered from stonehenge to broken circle/spiral hill. both spring from the same basic desires—and serve the same function. the comparison between these two earthworks have certainly been remarked upon previously. seeing them relatively one after the next was quite a wonderful thing. no matter how silly the idea of travelling a good distance to see an arrangement of rocks and earth, the presence of this place means something to me that is beyond logic. long lost feelings and desires are somehow activated at these sites. it's the same when in front of a good painting, no matter how absurd museums become as depositories for them. somehow quite like the feeling when you're sitting around a fire just watching the embers glow. sensing the moon, wondering about everything in general.

PURGE!

All in one dream that sees me fit:
I fit into you
I love yr flowery heart
pumping blood over the heavens

I reap the wretched thing that talks
I am up! up!
on a wing
pressure on my skull
I reach for what I am
find no explanation
my mind a slippery thing
which snakes thru barbs
snagging
without rest
writhing thru the real.
shall I continue?

The mind is a thing that wants
my mind wants to see itself
shining in the light
but a fever pitches thru
rolls around inside
there is no light inside
we must crack the skull!
pour on the hot oil!
we must open the mind!
let it bleed for you
(this thought an arrow
pinning yr cuff)

The mind flies!
we must crack the skull!
un-weight the lights!
singe the synapses
to creamily caress the cranial case!
will I continue?
I want an open flower
in this decaying yard
I want to see the bloom
before it fades, to wither

can eyes see "I"?
can I crack the skull?
will I continue?
shall I continue?
show me the flowers
shower me with flowers
show me the flowers
shower me with flowers
show me the flowers
shower me with flowers
purge!
purge!

Bad Moon Rising Tour: '85

19 may 85
akron, ohio

sleepy early morning sunshine in small town akron. people are just waking up, here as anywhere else. birds, etc. strong sun cuts through the shadow. nothing going on, just a small town along the roadside west. early summer here, and the road seems very inviting. anywhere from here would be an improvement. this nondescript sector of the eastern edge of the mid-west breeds a strange lazy day— no-one going anywhere fast, stop here for long and you might wake up in twenty years at sunday mass. so the road streams thru here like the river of salvation, a grey strip of asphalt embedded in the thick mind of the middle west. the trees hang with the unnatural stillness only found in the small towns of america. chrome car bumpers gleam in the bright morning parking lots and along curbsides. by the malls and motels tufts of grass mix with shards of broken glass bottles and pieces of worn out cardboard boxes. things to be ignored, we'll look the other way.

21 june 85
solstice

thom:
winding thru dark tunnels now on "A" train going home. saw some of the city today—just walked streets, sleeveless, in the hot summer sun—I FELT THE SUN— and hung out on hot corners, nowhere, watching it all. Houston St., 6th Avenue, 8th Ave., all real cool, a hot blister-village life as in hamlet-size. in this giant city-sphere yet!

How've you been?

SKIN OF LIFE

once again i find myself travelling across these corn fed plains, the hot sun beating down a deadly brightness, we're almost to Iowa, the clouds hang like a fleet of ships, and i find the same old despair cropping up (as Dr. P. said it would).

LIFE HAS NO SUBSTANCE. i find nothing to grip at the moment. everything seems to lie on the surface—how one looks, what things SEEM like. are there real indicators in this superficial skin of life? if so they elude me. i was not built for this surface level. i fail miserably here. *the skin of life.* i can see it but i don't believe it. *"i am nothing if not you."* we inform the same pool. on which post are you hung? the surface is all we see, how can it not matter?

remember: OBSESSION
REPRESSION
TRANSFORMATION
EMPATHY
ENTROPY

take now for instance: the late sun is casting long shadows thru the brilliant atmosphere. the corn glows. deep greens color endless fields, houses, a barn here, a few tall shade trees for solace. the sky is dense w clouds, a heavy blanket that falls back towards the edge of the world. knotted strings of shining electrical wires drape from pole to pole alongside us.

i see this around me, this outer skin. these elements can be found, it's not their individuality that i see. they are not unique. i see beyond clouds and thru bldgs and trees. i see the imprint of this landscape. the endless resignation, daily repetitions. things grown under hot sun. a static quality , a feedback cycle just like four electric gtrs laid on top of their full blast amps. a sound so loud it pushes into silence. FROZEN MOVEMENT. the skin of life would reveal a unique moment, but i do not believe in that moment. this view has been here forever, not unique but rather ordinary, beyond everyday, eternal—"i've lived here all my life."

the skin of life deceives me. it appears solid and yet there is nothing to grasp. people collect and shed the skins of various lives, filling their homes w art, collecting all sorts of knick-knacks and junk. trying to grasp life by its material bits, denying immateriality. denying mortality.

but there is nothing in life to touch, nothing to hold onto. shed your skin like a snake and slither off to die in the night. shed the skin of life. release yr hold on a dead dream. replace it w what? invent religion, or morality, or a chaos to fill the void.

the sun sinks pink over the vault of this day, making it harder to see but easier to feel. that's why the night is so right—the darkness insists that you feel, and fear, to move thru it.

don't believe in significance—things being containers for ideas and abstractions. these abstractions are feather-weight, barely tangible. many people believe that their lives are actually present, in front of them—that a beautiful girl is a beautiful girl—timeless—a frozen moment. there are no frozen moments. god!! the contradictions are insane!

today while on the road i found myself transported to the hillsides where golden grass enveloped me and bushy trees, dark green, swayed overhead in the shallow breeze. the pale yet deep blue of sky overhead. i could hear the cars on the interstate, and feel the dry and brittle grass beneath me. i wanted to be nowhere else, i wanted to sit under those trees, to feel the patchy shade and sun on my skin, and dream of nothing. right there as the sun made its beautiful bronze exit.

22 aug 85
LA

today in LA the sky was a cool deep blue and i could see the black of space behind pushing it into shape over my head. the clouds were plentiful and individual, keeping their distance from each other, each asserting its edges. HUNG overhead, completely motionless. the vault did not shift and glide heavy slo-throb over me, time was silent and no movement occurred. the sun beat hot but w a cool breeze. i craned my neck to see these phenomena—the sky was still over my head in West LA. it had stopped. even as cars drove by on Pico and the dogs barked and unsuspecting people w unlocked doors sat by the pools. (later at the radio interview these events were denied.)

that moment of the sky's silent halt was so ephemeral, so out of reach. i was looking at a moment imploding upon itself, a sealed room, closed circuit. that is how i recall LA.

august 1985
oregon to LA to norman, oklahoma

Some Excerpts:

A.
when we travelled thru southern oregon in the hot summer of August 1985 we found ourselves upon one of the most perfectly timeless landscapes i have ever seen—golden ochre hills rolling as far as one could see—glinting like polished brass. an occasional tree of dark navy-blue/green and the deep and pale blue of the sky, cloudless, pure, hung over the whole thing. a freshly paved blacktop road snakes its way through the landscape and the colors all gleam and buff against each other—deep black on golden yellow meets cerulean sky punctuated w

green. so vast and unforgettable, unphotographable. have to stand before it to believe it. . . .

B.
last night in idaho we looked out at the stars—i hadn't seen so many in a number of years. the days and nights here have been the clearest i've experienced anywhere; the whole milky way was visible and just to stand beneath its dome was transcendent. certainly the lack of stars overhead serves to suppress certain (essential) thoughts in city dwellers.

C.
a story where the landscape itself is seen as the main protagonist evolving over vast periods of time, with the human population fleeting like specks over the surface—ants on a tabletop. how would humanity be perceived by the living planet?

after a couple thousand years pollution would cause changes in ecological growth patterns, the transmutation of elements into asphalts and plastics will have some effect, but in light of a 4 million year history can the events of a few millennia mean very much?

maybe the earth barely notices these things—just waits patiently for the future to slowly unfold on the past, for the hurtling stars to slow to a halt, across infinite distances, and begin to turn inwards again, time reversing.

D.
well another beginning here. we're in LA now, the city of angels which i love. it's a false front—all trimmed neat and cinematic, clean yet it will suck you under. a dark haired woman, kohl around the eyes. staring at me.

last night we went to visit some LA friends and hung around. some guy who is subletting carmel's place (where we were) picks a stoned-out paranoid fight w this weird LA chick who looks like a cross between elvira and mortissia adams. it turns out that the guy who was subletting as i said is a con artist and he was freaking out, saying angrily (he's english accented to boot) "I WANT THIS GIRL OUT OF THE APT. NOW!" and silenced all conversation in the apartment. later he tries to steal someone's pot-stash and rip some cash off someone else. totally weird, a totally LA paranoid high-school-esque scene, all of us wondering whether he would pull a gun or knife any moment, and do a full scale LA acid-cityscape-cliche-ridden freak out. felt like i was back ten years ago at some high-school party at elise langbaum's parent's house up on the hill.

this is LA and i like being here, it's the alternate side, a different evolution from NYC along the same "deep dark city" lines we first heard about in sci-fi novels—"a teeming uncontrollable snowball in the drifts of civilization."

E.
little pools of shade beneath the trees. the bales are stacked in the hot sun which is like an unbelievable drug. dust flies, we end up behind two ancient and dusty dumptrucks carrying gravel and leaving a thick stream of particles in the air. voices have been replaced here by lge. billboards, which speak thru the hot sun. a carny sets up tents on the flat field of golden grass. the circus is in town. hot town, hot time tonite. we'll send you out in the fields at night, under the full moon hanging and thousands of stars, tiny spears to the eye. or down by the red river at dawn when mist hangs, just before the heat of day. the barn boards splinter and crumble of their own volition in this heat. gray, crumbling bldgs stand in link w the new. why tear down anything here where there is so little? given its chance, the sun would erase all history. so we let our heritage stand. we look back on youth. the fields roll, the clouds roll across them. i can see for miles, there's no-one in sight.

F.
yes we're past the deep SW of cacti and sage. now in the underbelly of the heartland—Tx/Okla border, where the golden grasses climb flat lands with just a trace of roll. skies here are miles wide, and the big birds swoop and glide for hours on the lazy currents. the air is brilliant, crisp and in hard focus. every detail etches on the retina, threatening to burn on thru. endless farmlands—all huge and (yes!) privately owned. the trees hang, the telephone poles, the sun, the Sun, the SUN!! over a rise i go. little pools of shade beneath the trees!

53

31 aug 85

ENROUTE

enroute thru Missouri,
Illinois and now Kentucky
on to Atlanta thru
the 3 AM hazy
moonglow night.
finally the visions
have come: LA and after
tumbling one upon the next.

1 sept 85
pennsylvania

so this guy follows me into the men's room at a gas station somewhere in southern P.A. it's around the side with old rusty cars sitting permanently in the grass behind the place. he pulls in behind us and follows me in. muttonchops, moustache almost fu-manchu, balding in the center of his head, the indefinable middle age that could be thirty-five or fifty. not young at all, not technically old. first, he can't get the soap dispenser to work—he doesn't realize he has to pull this lever underneath the box. then he can't get the water to go on—it's one of them "modren" faucets w just one center knob that you pull for flow and twist for temp.

"now what the hail. . . ."

me: "you've got to pull it."

"well how about that, things're changing so fast you can't keep up. next thing you know these faucets will be talkin' to ya. . . . they'se the coke machines that do that, d'ya ever run accrost one of those?"

me: "one of what?"

"them coca-cola machines that talk back to ya. scared me clear to hail."

me: "no i've never run across one."

"really! they've got two over in Shambersburg."

he moves into the stall, his hands finally clean and dry. he keeps talking as i move to exit.

"yes, i'm telling you soon they'll have cars that'll steer themselves. you won't have to drive 'em at all . . . just hafta sit there. . . ."

i couldn't believe it. on the road we're passing farms w silos and lots of corn. we're almost to three-mile island territory. i can feel its radioactive heartbeat gaining strength.

27 oktober 85
london

can i steal a few minutes to write? amanda just stepped out, cody is asleep before me on the floor. he takes so much of our collective time that little is left over. it's late afternoon on a cloudy sunday in london. so far things here have been pretty good. the apts. are serviceable if small, and the weather has been crisp and clear, allowing us to spend the better part of each day out roaming the city, which is fairly beautiful and interesting to me right now.

cody is growing up, as if by magic. even since we've been here i can see the changes in his little countenance. he's gaining control over his physical movement, a little more all the time, and he has now a real personality—he's no longer (already! at four months) a helpless flopping entity; now he is a real person. i actually realized this the other night when i came home late to find he and amanda already asleep in the flat. there were two people in the room! i slipp'd down to the floor to watch him sleeping and breathing for a few minutes. watch him roll and stretch, fix his face when he was pressed straight into the covers so he wouldn't smother himself. his little body was alert and watching over his well being; it took a bit of the worry off my shoulders to see that in some ways he could already take care of himself.

now when awake he is quite observant and playful—when we're out in the city or with other people his eyes are wide—he's taking in everything. i wonder what he'll retain of these early sightings, and in what manner. his powers of observation seem quite acute, i sense a good deal of as yet unstructured intelligence behind his beautiful eyes, he's trying to make sense of things, even though he has yet to build up the structures which will allow him to do so. he's pure now, his body still in control for the most part, his mind has not yet taken over, he's in that lucky state of grace, before the world comes crashing in upon his head. now he's one with his world, there is no separating from it, even though he doesn't know this. i almost dread for him the day ahead when he first sees himself as separate from it. that's when the problems of living creep in, even as it is a time of great revelation. one sees oneself as an individual, capable of things which will set one apart from everyone else, make one somehow special. ah! the cause both of life's pleasures, self sufficient, powerful, and pains, lonely and isolated. he has a long way to go. hope i'll be there for him. IN IT/OUT OF IT/(IN IT AGAIN) things in london are winding to a close. amanda and cody left yesterday. we've played our last (and best) gig here and now there are only two days left.

strange forebodings have been w me on this tour. images of death and dying have been haunting me. when i was ill in europe i thought i was dying. now my father has had a heart attack, nicholas' father dies. it seems all in all a very weird time.

we had another endless interview today. this w a very effete and intellectual pair, very british, who kept wanting to know "what do you mean by this song." they don't understand that music is innate, it thrives in a dark air of mystery and emotion, mysticism and intuition. it is something that *moves one* first and foremost; when over-analyzed it becomes dry and lifeless. we do not try to pinpoint what we do, we leave it open and rely on collective intuition to make it happen. we lean outwards towards infinity by leaving the things open-ended.

it is a politics of small spheres, of individuals rather than groups and of multiplicity. the world is fragmented and we see the pieces. they form a loosely knit whole, some teetering semblance of image, yet w gaps large enough for things still to fall thru. because one can never cover every base at once. chunks of matter will always fall through. tiny idea-lettes will sift thru like sand thru a wire mesh. we battle time, we battle the constraints of limits.

the only way to maintain a forward momentum (as opposed to a static image-face) is to keep free of pinpoint type thoughts—we are free to see into the future through the past, to move in a world where ideas slip and scud over each other in some theoretical version of the continental plate tectonics. sometimes two or more plates will align, and a pearl of truth will drop through the mesh. if so that is grand.

one is a finite body, yet the last thing to want is a hard and frigid unchanging mind. ideas float, they rise up thru the open air and drift freely in and out of sight.

on NYC music in general:

it is almost defiantly about individuality. you never find that NY bands make music others could "cover," but rather the opposite, that only those making this music could do so. it steps back and away from the tradition of continuity in music history, covering tracks behind itself, insisting on a here and now, in sound, that is about the lives that construct it, more so than about a common idiom. the extreme NY music insists on individuality at the expense of all else, including intelligibility sometimes. (no-wave and beyond.) i think we ride that fence (S.Y.).

19 nov 1985
kobenhavns

late morning now, here in copenhagen—the skies cold and heavy with snow about to fall, the windows running w. condensation. we've been here a couple of days, carlos and moniek are with us, and we are all waiting under the cast-iron sky. already london england seems quite far away, although i was faced w that familiar melancholy upon the final leaving of the flat, empty now, without amanda, the tv, or cody stretching up his head from the floor to look at me. put it all behind me, now it's all behind me, memory places it in the rapidly receding recesses of my mind, like looking in the rear view mirror along the grey interstate. the rear view mirror, a good equation for memory, looking forwards and yet somehow seeing backwards; that is the pain of memory.

denmark strikes me very similar to the flat landscape of holland. i expected copenhagen to be quite awesome in beauty and northern-arctic-romance, but it's actually just another grey city, cold weather blanketing streets that could be anywhere—zurich, linz, vienna, anywhere in europe.

in contrast to my romantic notion, we have found kids w dirty clothes and leather jackets and dirty faces, leading us through the streets and talking of combating the high costs here through the thrift of theft. living in squalid squats w apple computers and video rigs <<hot>> stashed under their beds. partially completed fancy stereo systems.

i suppose that in the end our little lives are not in danger of harm or robbery, despite slight warnings and a ripple of paranoia; we'll end up doing our gigs, reaching out to touch the scandinavian consciousness, twice, and then crawl onwards to Brussels and finally touch down home in NYC, barring any unforeseen problems in the air, nomads no more. for awhile.

paul mccartney has just come on the turntable, his sweet mess trying to banish these grey thoughts, to push them across the skies. the dishes are being done, the cats are crawling in and out of the chair legs in this room, everyone is finally getting up—well, steve is being forced up now by carlitos. "the world is waiting for you" he tells him, "yeah i know" is the despondent reply. it seems not even the world waiting is earthshaking enough to supplant dreams of sleep/vision.

19 novembre 1985
KOBENHAVNS

half a mile from the RR tracks

half a mile from the RR tracks and i'm takin' it jack, w a gun in my back.
half a mile from the end of time i get off the line.
step over the first stone, i stutter on the street, stand by the water, out on the bridge. that's how i'm carried over, by this bridge which turns me out as i cross it. i'm grey. it's a grey day and the streets rush up. we walked in copenhagen—*koben-havns*—today, cold and it snowed. colder than it's been, colder than i've been, and brisk like the sea is brisk, an icicle inhaled. we saw pictures that were NoWhErE, man, all greybrown and in duplication, except for *The Window,* thru which, no not really thru which but rather by which i was transported. (really.) later the real pic came in a cafe on some main street in town, full of smoke and whisky bottles

alongside delicious shiny *danisher* fruit pies. coffees going by . . . run by a pakistani who had been to new york. the girl behind the counter was blonde on blonde, all white. all right. he called me "newyork" and "hey holland, free coffee on the house" to moniek and carlos. the girl had (an absolutely DANISH countenance, what else would be possible?) icy white skin shaping a face which captivated me, rung by golden blonde and a white "serving coat" over her sheer black blouse, just a hint of deep dark black in an otherwise vision in white, the picture that wasn't on the wall, but standing before me. i couldn't stop looking, i couldn't stop thinking, no thinking allowed. the pakistani called out to tell us of a trip to NYC, once: "two thousand dallars in my pocket on forty-second street and i couldn't look at no one. so i called up the girl in boston who told me to take the shuttle up from JFK (husker du?) which i did, and wow, what a beautiful city!" the girl kept coming into view and i wantedtotakeherpicturebut couldn't really ask her somehow and knew anyway that it would only be a picture of a vision, which is really nothing at all. so i have had to file her away in my memory instead, which i have done, with a great final image of nearly following her out the door as we were leaving and her shift had ended and she was leaving too. but that's one dream too far. . . .

later we were confused by the dark and the cold and the water-at-night. . . . ran into a dutchman, and no-one else, not even the ducks again, on the street home. these streets hold everything in, not reflecting like any kind mirror or pool, there are no shiny reflections here of any kind, everyone is holding everything in.

logic seeps through the floorboards
no-one keeps score, no-one is counting
records are all strewn about
i'm leaving now. thank you.

20 nov 85
kobenhavns

postcard to jeff

this place, which i had romanti-fantasized as a beautiful mythic place is actually among the more uninteresting and straight-laced places i've been. a land on the edge of civilization, last to get the news, the most grey and traditional. i suspect (still) that deep in the heart of scandinavia lay beautiful mysteries cradled deep amongst the fjords. i shall not see them this time. the folks here, and especially our girl-waitress in a bar, have beautiful pale deprived-of-sun skin, thin like pearls, almost transparent. this one girl—no, woman—was white skin and gold hair, white clothes; a vision, an opalescent danish beauty.

it snowed today, wet and grey, cold and brisk. tomorrow we go to malmo, sweden, then to brussels and home.

21 nov 85
before the light

somehow i've grown to hate the night here, these dark hours w nothing to do and all talked out, not a thing to manipulate or play with, just a room w beautiful long floorboards. large enough and empty enough to feel empty. it's 4 AM all copenhagen is asleep yet our candles are burning still; the waxy smell mingles w the smoke and sweet saints. i don't want to sleep it is a robbery to me right now yet the whole house lays bare. it's a comforting room, where *nothing* can become an occupation, w ease. so far this city is only seen in relation to others, not as a thing in itself. maybe it's these endless nights that are its true character. i wonder if it's what Edvard Munch felt, his skull pressing in.

it sometimes seems as though some of the best thinking time comes while staring out the window of a moving vehicle. right now it's a train, come from kobenhavns and just left hamburg and carlos and moniek behind, in the drifts of one of the first of the winter snows.

it's late at night and the large flakes drift thru the street lamp-lit pools of light, bright and rainbow like. even the train man stands in the corridor for a long stretch watching the skiens of track pass, covered in a growing coat of white, and the lonely roads w o a soul on them, passing in the night. here and there a window glows w. a warm yellow incandescence; the glow of the parlor lamp has replaced that of the hearth.

the empty streets and cold chill of the snowy weather take me somewhere that can't be described in words. sometimes it is a feeling of the infinite, of knowing the cold winter snows will always come, year after year, w the purity of a cleansing breath, and the finality of things dying. i could feel very old if i thought about it, although not at all very wise. these scratches of my handwriting remind me of what i've seen of the writing of my parents and grandparents, even something as simple as handwriting is perpetuated, handed down thru time. will cody's handwriting some day mirror this page too? if i don't think about the past or the future, what is left? the present is either full of things to occupy time, or else as silent as an empty room. i can not stop the thoughts which speed thru my mind, i am helpless and follow them wherever they go. i can't shut it out or shut it off, i can't let the mental processes come to a halt like the train comes down. lately the nights have been an endless struggle to shut off the flow. in the days the thoughts, or words, force their way out w o control. stray objects or notions, a color, a place, falling snow etc. can click, a chain of images which come pouring forth. from where do they actually come? i am no closer to answering that question than i ever was. is this akin to speaking in tongues? what is profound? what is really real? i sometimes feel as if my whole life is an endless defeat, having accomplished nothing of consequence, having come no closer to any truths. in all the activity of a tour like this, the very notion of truth seems further from reality than ever. nothing seems too real except the feeling of movement. so the gentle rhythm of the train is much more than a comfort. in some ways it is the only indication of life in an otherwise empty frame.

10 may 86
london

utrecht set

inhuman
shadow of a doubt
starpower
death to our friends
death valley '69
secret girl
tom violence
white kross
expressway

---

world looks red
marilyn moore

eight a.m. now and england is over. traveling thru the early morning sunlight of holland, off the boat, out over the flat lands en route to eindhoven. there has been so little time this trip. three weeks in england w one week in holland, gone by in a blur of roads and one club after another, one vice leading to the next.

england was all business this trip. even the pleasure was business-like. europe, and holland especially, is much more comforting and contemplative, although not *alive* in the same way as london, which is hustle bustle like NYC, but w more access to the machinery of things than in NY, for us.

maybe it had to do w being on a train again. since our first trips over we've done more driving than train riding. the motorways are good in some respects, but they also provide such a familiar feeling, whereas the trains seem more exotif in comparison.

so much seems to have happened this last month. another season has drifted by, i saw the buds open in new york and the flowers bloom in england. feelings of mortality come and go, increasing intakes of assorted stimulants alter any sense of routine and exchange for it an unending madness of sorts, an unreality where anything might happen, a timeless zone where nothing happens. across the line where dreams and waking experiences meld in a kind of cinema of the mind. nothing less possible than anything else. presently, for instance, i am hovering over a body of golden water, suspended like a plane over clouds. it's not impossible, my eyes are open.

accomplishment is its own reward. i walk thru a dream punctuated by various exorcisms of my soul. they will be all that's left one day.

now the time will fly by, in a mad dash across europe. each image rising and falling on the screen in succession. none lasting, none real other than in the moment.

1 may 86
venezia, near treviso

in italy again, the early morning bright sunshine transforms this place from a dark mystery into a peaceful walk thru another era. this place is so foreign. the pace of life so varied here that it is hard for us to adjust to it. i sense an amount of disdain amongst us for the things which go on here. i dislike feeling this way. this place has such a familiar aspect to me, whether it be the tone of conversations, bubbling along in this beautiful and expressive tongue, or just seeing some family members outside a house, talking, walking in their sunday church-going clothes along the paths by their washing all hung out in the dry sunshine. the scraggly green plants everywhere. somehow i feel a real unity w all of this place.

i am transported to my childhood, to brooklyn and the big family gatherings there. then, twenty–thirty years ago, the pull of this culture was very strong in my own extended family. all the children, the aunts uncles wine-drinking bocci games, a great deal of the old country in that life. i suppose in many ways it ends w me and the others of my generation. finally the old ways are seen merely as archaic, and no longer as a part of the warp and woof of life. it took three generations, i can call myself "american" fairly safely. although i still have shadowy memories of an italian heritage the language is now gone, the great big families, even the home cooked tomato sauces are going. i suppose when cody is older there will be not a hint of this culture left; he will have to deal w the bland homogenization of america. i had seen such a situation as a blessing, yet now it suddenly appears a curse.

yet there's no point in holding on artificially to something from the past. when things like this are gone that's it. growing up for me, there was too much to take in that was new, the old culture appeared dusty and like a faded object on a shelf. it was only years later that such objects became appealing to me, and by then the original pieces of my heritage were almost gone, i was left to substitute for them the discarded debris of any old flea market treasures which came along—any of these photo albums could have meaning for me. who knows? maybe some parts of the past are so deeply ingrained that they will remain part of cody's makeup in spite of the white, milk-fed culture he is growing into. after all, he's got a russian

65

past to think about as well as italian. he's a child of the globe, only possible in this modern age.

2 june 86
aix-en-provence

how incredible. the early morning sun is streaming down golden, radiant on the stones of the houses of france. incredible, to wake up in Cezanne's town and have not a minute to visit w him as we steam across the entire southern perimeter of france, speeding past the riviera late yesterday, and now to leave aix-en-pce this morning to race past arles, avignon, the entire landscape of french impressionism passing before my eyes. the air heavy w blues and greens, bright cadmium reds and yellows. ochre bldgs w violet shadows everywhere. this pedestrian landscape, so simple looking, is stalked by the ghosts of mythic figures. i feel them press my shoulder and shake hands. but time, or its lack, insures that we do not speak.

june 86
NL, entoute to groningen

along the dikes-hiway

there's too much weather, and too little light. we're traveling along the edge of the world right now, overcast and wet, hiway glistening, mist rising off it. the few patches of green are soiled, muddy, unsuitable. the ocean is pushing against the barricades, we're on both sides surrounded. the air in the van is turgid, gravid (pregnant), PSI increasing. oncoming headlights whizz by w alarming proximity. will the dikes hold? the wind is whipping up the brew. sheep on the leeward banks, standing dumb, stretched for miles (km). the poor beasts, they bear the weight of the sins of the world.

last night in the dark interior of the club i sat deep in the dark in a thick brown leather holster. i brought a hand to my forehead—the room anechoic, dust rising thru the silent conversations, nothing audible amidst the din and shuffling movement.

that finger ran a cross on my skin, traced the true cross on my forehead. why? what does it mean? thru what manner of transmission does it hold some mysterious meaning for me? is it thru ancient myths, or some word-picture which struck me as a child? without knowing why this movement was/is significan't, i found myself stunned by the power of its thought/form. my mind was emblazoned w a fiery brand, etched along the synapses. this secret myth-image came and went within seconds, and yet i feel it crouched, days behind me, waiting to spring.

the entire world right now—all i see (that is the entire world)—is held in some tightening vise behind the cloud cover. blue-grey black and tightening, tightening. we can none of us wrench free from this place. we have to ride it out.

23 june 1986
virginia

leaving friendly richmond virginia now, wonderful little town of one long street— Broad St.—with all life coming and going from there. dying factories and typical american turn-of-the-century architecture. a town going nowhere, and in no hurry to boot. we're heading south, onward, the smell of tobacco coming off the fields and the Phillip Morris factories belching cancerous smoke.

let's leave behind the last two getting-under-way days and move into the american landscape. petty concerns will knock you out of the water on a journey like this.

so far the gigs (Wash/Philly/Richmond) have been good in spite of both major and minor fuckups every night. we've been up and down from NY to DC and then back up thru Baltimore again to Philly, and i think somehow we're glad to get out of the loop of that repeating stretch of rte. 95. it felt like we were travelling w o getting anywhere. now we're truly on the way and it's just turned summer and it' hot Hot HOT, there's no turning back.

in this time of much traveling the visions of the hiway have gradually changed shape—dulled in a way, quite frankly, and there seems to be nothing special about each place we come to—life is going on, it's not a big deal, we're a transitory element in an otherwise stable environment. we are what goes, what comes by and moves on.

so far we've been maintaining a surprisingly even keel, w no intoxicants short of some beer drinking. it's nice to feel good and healthy traveling, as opposed to completely over the top out on the edge.

the other night we unwittingly found ourselves staying in a porn motel outside of baltimore, run by orientals w a two-hour rate, etc. what an incredible slice of the seamy tacky side, w couples pulling up and pulling off w amazing regularity. for the most part the movies were boring and poorly made, no plots, overdubbed moan tracks.

23 june 86
later, close to raleigh, NC

just finished reading *less than zero* and it started out stupid but ended up alright, a very conventional book, actually. by the end i didn't hate it anymore. there's a section where he's sitting in his old grade-school yard watching kids playing and another section about the death of his grandmother from something or other. both of those were pretty evocative.

getting old and having life really begin to seep away: how sad it is, how normal. i hate the thought of it, how tragic and unstoppable. i'd like to ask my mother what it feels like, but i wouldn't know how to broach the subject. it's a long way off for me to think about death, by old age at least, and yet i can feel the deterioration of the body and i get a sickly feeling.

gram parsons is singing now on the box, long dead, his body dug up and stolen from out amongst the joshua trees and desert flowers. many of the people who have influenced me (books, etc.) are dead and somehow the tragic nature of their deaths (Kerouac, Fassbinder, Hemingway, so many, Elvis . . .) seem to be a large part of their importance. the ones whom it seemed could feel the end, the futile aspect of life, right from the word go. who struggled to continue and create (Schiele) in spite of the realization that they would end up in the tragic soul-less air. of course there's no point in not continuing, for then you're stuck unable to move a step.

if one wants ultimately to proceed we must choose life, choose activity, the world, creation. but always tempered by the black cloud and by the sense that time is finite for us all, no matter how we seek infinity. it's a concept, a dream that has no end. we seek a land without limit, we seek everlasting hope.

9 or 10 july
portland

just met an old coot on the streets, gray hair and handlebar mustache, black cowboy hat and turquoise tie, he was drunk i guess and had a paper bag in one hand and a transistor radio in the other and was talkin' something about cops and FBI detectives and the electric chair but i couldn't understand a word he said, except that he had the most incredible northwestern drawl which just rolled out of his mouth like a popsicle.

last night we arrived at the giant groves of redwoods just as the sun was fading, night approaching any moment. it was incredible—we walked out among the trees, the light gone completely, no moon and we all walked in. the trees towered up, shadowy hulks that just stretched up forever, the beautiful textured bark twisting, spiraling around the trunks, you could see the trees pushing up out of the earth, stretching high, on a time scale we can't even come close to comprehending. the ferns on the ground and giant cathedral ceilings overhead created a most incredible atmosphere. there seemed to be no animal life at all, no birds, no rodents, it was eerie how silent it was.

at one point we came upon a huge giant which had fallen over, giant root base sidewise and gnarly as hell. we climbed up the side of the truck onto the top of the tree and walked its entire length of 100 yards or so—all in the incredible pitch. we must have been ten or fifteen feet off the floor on top of this tree walking in the ruts of the bark, dark as though walking blindfolded. towards the end the interior was rotted out, and we were walking on top of a hollow core. the tree had died, expired, and you could sense it walking the trunk-side. the bark felt soft in comparison to that of a living tree, almost as if it was turning to dirt under our feet, turning to dirt and earth. in a couple of places branches which had been limbs were now growing straight up and using the dead trunk as the earth on which they grew. the giant tree returning to particles of earth.

eventually, after almost getting lost, we wound up back at the cars and had to go onwards, but i just didn't want to leave those woods. jeff and i lingered behind the others, standing on the barely visible path, looking up to see trees against dark sky—the most vivid contrast in a land of otherwise ghostly shadows all soft focus, soft edged. there were no endings or beginnings, each form melted into the next. darkened chiaroscuro. finally we had to leave, there was no point in lingering any further.

there are lightning storms all around us now, in the blue dark, bursts of energy behind the distant clouds. somehow it mirrors my current state, i feel as though there are deep things brewing beneath the surface, swelling and fading like volcanic activity. Lennon said "say what you mean, make it rhyme, and put a beat to it." right now in the dark of the fields and silos of kansas, it seems like good advice.

kids in houses crawl across their floors and dance w shaggy hair. the moon is up and no immediate danger is on the horizon. we make love on couches and sit talking in corners. if the cops come we smile and ask them to leave. a girl w dark hair and darker eyes, too too young to be real comes over w her plaid shirt. she can't say much, she's a good girl and already bored w her place in life, restless to see what's to come. ready to push things over. she can sit and let the music wash over her, or laugh hysterically while waving her arms wildly. but these things aside she can merely wait for this life somehow to end, and for something else to take its place. she can choose whom she wants to be with, and she doesn't really have to worry about it. her young body is perfect, always willing and she lies there anyway, and lets it wash over. she has the power. her innocent dark eyes don't deny it. she sits and waits, bored by the boys around her, and their boy-scenes. a picture of her would be old and useless the minute it surfaced, she changes by the minute. it's a long way to go till she knows of women and children but for now she can sit, her legs widely straddling the whole fucking world because she's got the power she's got the beauty and the sex her body is perfect you only need touch her to know it. she is all around the world, w a knowing glance. she is the world— whole/secure/lying in wait.

well this is indianapolis, indiana home of the speedway kings and i can see why no-one knows much else about this place. it's all red-brick factories and kids hangin' out sitting on car hoods in parking lots up the street or out along the edge of the hiway where at this time of the night you can hear 'em shiftin' gears through the streets. that high whining sound comes over the trees. i love this place tonight. it has nothing but a full moon to recommend it. the streets lay flat on the land in between the corn fields and the buildings, those old neo-victorian rundown beautiful, once beautiful bldgs. next to stone factory/office atrocities of square brick, square box. i know this place somehow, it's ingrained in my memory yet it's been in hiding, forgotten behind some wall there. i seem to have suppressed it, or just forgotten: now it's only known in corny story song versions of spring-steen/mellencamp (he didn't come to the gig) and the lesser known worser off of their ilk. those guys are okay, they've just had their vision blown up to the point where every joe on the street has heard it, and ignores it.

these streets and trees wind thru the center of the town, the red brick factories run down and on the long road out kill me—the same ones as binghamton and every other city east of the mississippi. those big windows so sad w the glass running down the panes (glass a liquid, supercooled).

i remember driving around parking lots in oyster bay w kids older than me who had souped up 442's or Roadrunners, Chevy Novas or Dodge Chargers—i wasn't particularly interested in the speed or the danger (too sure it will be my way out) but anyway it was something to check out w all the lingo of hurst's and headers and chrome mags. spinning donuts in empty parking lots just for the fuck of it. i'd ride but could never figure out where these guys actually thought they were gonna go.

just hanging out in the parking lot tonight brought all that back, trying to tell carlos how in some manner summer in america equates (in some way) to sitting around on car hoods, bull-shitting in the heat of parking lots somewheres out among the cooling buildings at night. i can feel it still, etched. just go cool away in the spree. dig stars, orion's up.

we drove thru town and in the center was a giant war memorial which rose up big and bulky full of columns like some giant boxy inept version of the acropolis or something. it was hideous and wonderful.

you can't hold onto these streets where experiences happened. you can just look at each town as it goes by and wonder, if it had been here how it would've went down and what would have been the same, what different. what form would the myth take here? i'm sure from the look of this place, and the people we met at the gig, who were wild and open, that it has its own special stamp.

23 july 86
buffalo

after driving well into the dawn last night w Dinosaur trailing, looking for a cheap motel. today we're all a bit burned out. we did have some fun on the road this morning as we pulled onto the hiway, throwing things at each others' cars (bibles, bottle rockets, cassette tapes smashing on the hiway) and Dinosaur almost got totally blown away by a giant semi which roared up from behind while we were playing swerving-lane-games. it was a real eye opener.

we went to visit niagra falls which was alright but not as i remember it. it's entirely surrounded—this bit of roaring blue and green—by parking lots. pitiful.

tonights' show went okay. we rocked hard although the PA was shitty. Dinosaur were great although not as awesome as last night. i sang neil young's "cortez the killer" w them which was a lot of fun. those guys are really great; j especially is pretty weird and easy to talk to. we watched some videotape which relived the other days psychedelic experience, it was pretty "tripped out." carlos in a heavy giggle.

i met paul sharits the filmmaker tonite after the gig without knowing who he was at the time, and i took him for some kind of coked-out older dude w his sports jacket, wild print shirt open neck and gold chain, his talk of "having connections," but now i regret not knowing it was him. also met a fairly beautiful dark haired girl named kate or kay whom i barely talked to but who was just great.

it's late and my ears are ringing again.

1 august 86
boston

MOST POPULAR U.S. SET ORDER

tom violence
white kross
-tape-
shadow of a doubt
starpower
death to our friends
i love her all the time
secret girls
brother james
expressway

---

marilyn moore

goodbyes have been said, the whole thing is unloaded, everything put away and sorted. carlos leaves tomorrow, thurston and kim leave today. only steve will be left in ny for the summer.

there's too long a stretch behind to begin to reflect upon now; somehow this morning i thought of those first days in the US, when carlos came and we were fixing up the van, readying to leave. it seems a long way from there to the onerous asshole i became at times in the last moody week, arguing stupid points w my favorite dutchman. but i suppose all has been chalked up to road-weariness, we had a great final reflective talk last evening about the trip and the future and america and everything. we parted like brothers still and i'm real glad of that as he's "one of the best."

the coming month has me wondering what will be. i'd really like to spend some time getting down some of the many things that've come to me this last month or so, yet i know it would be an immense task—if i sit to start typing it's going to be quite a lengthy process. my thoughts right now are long and involved, too detailed to come out in a succinct page or two.

the last three months have been so busy, and have brought so many changes for the future—the last six months actually, since we started in on EVOL. there are going to be major changes for me in daily life now, w o a job, more time for my work, and i'm really looking forward to pushing ahead.

we're riding the border of lake erie right now, it's far below thru the haze and beautiful; we're following the coastline and once again i'm in the air—moving across america.

ENTERING S CAROLINA

NOW   NOW   NOW

FLAMING TELEPATHS TOUR 1986

10/31/86

Halloween—first gig tonite, fIREHOSE is on now, we're deep in the woods of new york state and the stars are out in full force. looking up to the heavens i see something i otherwise miss. the stars take me out of this state. like always the first day-getaway was a mess and we drove late into the evening to make time and came very late anyway, but also like always it didn't matter.

11/1/86

morning broke hard with a false alarm on the fire bell. we stumbled around in the hotel lobby, eyed suspiciously by the security guards. the gig was a mess but we got through and we're in the country again and the leaves are red and now we're really heading out.

late afternoon now and the sky is about to fade, the rain washing down the night. now it's the taillights that are red, and the leaves invisible to me. we left watt at newark. mike was a crank and was already dreading his mates calling him for hanging out w we "bourgeoise"; but then they're econo, wouldn't understand the hotel or getting some sleep and getting out a bit refreshed. but then again they're also sitting in pittsbg., just hanging, and he's at godforsaken NEWARK wondering to himself. it's the first real night on the road now and it glistens wet like a fine rep-tile (i have heard tell . . .). we swerve forwards. . . .

it's fairly late now and we're still on the road in pennsylvania. it's dark and i can see nothing except the vs. beautiful shape of the road in front of us. it's deep depth-charge black with fresh-painted lines. the road is special to me, yet i can't convey the feeling, it has to be understood. so as metaphor the road has run free of me. i know how it feels, and i love the feeling, but i can't transmit it.

11/2/86

right NOW it's morning in middle america. i can't escape from it, and the trees whiz by and are mostly barren, all crisp and grey against the clear blue of sky. the grass still a pure green but w pools of dry leaves neath all the trees. like little rings. w fleks of red to complete the color scheme, and orange. it's the most colorful and soulful time now. i just love it. "Baby I Love You" by the Ronnettes is on the AM radio and it's such a great song, there's almost nothing in the world like a great song, esp. with dried cornfields and yello leaves for accompaniment.

11/3/86

we drove all through the night from ann arbor in the bleak and creaking, swaying van. st. louis came not too far into the day, earlier than so we're all in motel rms. trying to crash in the middle of the afternoon, with the red leaves and riverboats.

11/4/86

we're in columbia, missouri now. it's pretty cold here in the club and firehose are just about to go on. it's been wet and rainy all day but we did get to spend some time in a cool record store in st. louis. watt rode w us today and the van ride was t. rex blue oyster cult janet jackson and the beastie boys. oh yes and a long blast of the who w mike giving the blow by blow throughout. there were red leaves covering the sidewalks today, all soggy and splashy but it was nice to walk about outside on some small streets. real cool nowheresville smalltown. susanne's boots clinking along on the wet cement. we gave the promoter from last night some of the money back today because he was straight with us and lost quite a bit. he had to sell his vcr in consequence.

it seems like we've been out a long time but i know it's only been a few days so far. i'd like to be so much more descriptive about the sights but there's just been no time to do much besides what there's barely time to do. (sights vs. visions, hmmm.) i realized that one of the reasons i've found myself so attracted to landscape, and moved by it is that somehow the shapes are signif. to me, just looking at them. the land and the roadways cutting through— something really strong and permanent is here. i can't explain it any more than that tonight.

11/5/86

it's late now, i'm exhausted. we played tonite at the Outhouse, a "club" in the middle of a cornfield, miles from anywhere. another gig that was changed to a new location at the last minute. down dark dirt roads and over abandoned old railroad crossings to get here through the darkest of midwestern oklahoma star-field grain-fed crunch-dry frost-bite nights. it was cold and clear with plenty of stars— orion, etc—watching over us. fIREHOSE rocked; we all played to be warm. pretty uneventful. not what it should have been, but the dried out old cornfield was kinda nice anyway.

11/6/86

we are leaving norman, oklahoma now. this place is the end of the civilized world and it's the middle of the night and we weave along the highway.

so much has gone down. we're in florida now. desolate, dilapidated florida with old rotten billboards and boarded up shells of shattered enterprises. it's amazingly hot here, and the skies are broad and filled with dull, scrabbly clouds, although the sunsets we've seen let you know you're in the tropics again. texas is behind us and was the highlight of the trip, i think. the show in austin was the best, good crowd, we really rocked. liberty lunch is a great club, probably one of my favorites in the country at this point. with its half enclosed, half open to the sky format it's really special. daniel johnston came and we met him. he's incredible. the buttholes came too. texas, and austin in particular, feels so comfortable. people are really interested in the music and up for turning out to party and groove and listen. so different from some areas where the people don't seem to know why they've even come to the show, like last night in tallahasse. the show in san antonio with the buttholes was also really rockin' for us, maybe not quite as good as austin. we stayed at the house gibby, paul and jeff live in. it's pretty cool with their recording studio and a yard by the hiway. something that wouldn't be possible in new york city. they gave us a feast of great tex-mex food before the show which was fabulous. unfortunately for them, it wasn't the best of shows, they all seemed a bit bummed out by it—i don't know if it had to do with the fact that gibby did the promoting for it and had all that bullshit in his mind and just couldn't cut loose or what, but i guess we felt kinda bad that they did all the work and then didn't even have fun onstage.

next we're on an all nighter to baton rouge where we played in a k of c hall to a very small crowd, with the promoter whining all night about how much money he was going to lose. it was pretty throwaway, and we sucked. the only saving grace was during the encore when we covered watt with silly string during his bass solo. he looked like a rainbow-colored "cousin it."

another all nighter let us off in tallahasse last night for another show where the promoter was bummed and the people were weird and didn't much seem to care. sordid little club across the tracks, lots of pick-up scenes going on. felt like an old high school dance where everyone's got that hot summer-night need. someone for the night. the best part of the evening was the fact that dukowski had booked Saccharine Trust onto the bill as well. their tour is going in the opposite direction from ours, and meeting up was just great. they were in real good form and i loved watching their set. jack brewer is a god. the word seems to be that they may be calling it quits after this tour, and if that's so then this may have been the last Saccharine gig we'll see. that would be too bad. i can't understand how they can be this great band that's been around for so long and still be so under-appreciated.

we're heading to tampa now, almost there and with the sun going down. the skies are opening up; this is the second of five dates down here, and then the tour is about over.

11/12/86

we're travelling through the middle of florida. gainesville lies ahead. the landscape here is pretty wonderful, unique in its way from the whole u.s. quite a comparison to the two coasts, where the debris lies crumbling everywhere, old relics and testaments to the stupidity and greed of beachfront-hungry developers. central florida always evokes visions of africa, wide veldts with the suggestion of animals grazing and misshapen trees with spanish moss hanging down. after all, florida was once attached to africa, they're essentially of the same mold. the developers have mostly ruined the coasts here. what were once really amazing and wild places are now plastic, asphalt and brick, the ecology ruined. the mangroves have been uprooted on the coasts, but the interior holds little interest to the sun worshippers and has remained a bit freer. the everglades are still here. the long runs of coastline seem like a museum to misguided visions of thought. the whole thing—someday they'll give helicopter tours of each coastline, the atlantic tour and the gulf tour—melted from the heat, shapes deformed and fused into one giant bubbling and rusty heap, sitting on the sands. roofs caved in, piers lost to the sea. then the mangroves and the waterbirds will return to build nests on the balconies of rotted out, gutted condos. the sun here is so brilliant. . . .

11/13/86

spent the day travelling through the middle-lands of florida. what a great place—full of swampland and the feeling of someplace very old. stands of new pine trees next to dry grassland and cycad palms just beginning to top five feet tall. the sun beats down and the water from the sea has its fingers everywhere—trapped and stagnant, a primordial ooze and sludge, soaked full of algae and insects, all varieties of primitive life. we didn't get to swing by lake okeechobee because everyone is in a hurry and we really didn't have the time. even i had to admit it, although i wanted very much to go. i'd like to come back here in march with amanda and cody and do a photo expedition of these interiors. we didn't even come close to the everglades, or see much of the bird colonies, although now and then a small group of large black birds with beautiful wide wingspans would be hovering about, gliding on the air currents under the sun. what civilization there is here is just about as tragic as can be found. i find it fascinating and terrible—it's an entire culture warped out. but the land is just fine, one of the more enigmatic places in the country. dead zones where the bulldozers don't go.

11/14/86

T.SPIEL

What's up dude? It's been two weeks now for the FLAMING TELEPATHS tour. We've almost learned THE RED AND THE BLACK. I have to admit that our progress is nothing short of incredible! Same goes for STARPOWER. Both SONIC YOUTH and fIREHOSE playing together! But I have to confess that the road is hell for me and my head. Tonite is Jacksonville Beach in Florida (11/14/86), expecting shit of blow-out proportions. As always, I place myself into the hands of fate. What else?

love, mike

we head north from miami towards jacksonville now and in a few days back to new york city. i can't wait. miami was alright, we played in the district by the beach where all the art deco bldgs are and they were fine. otherwise we got there at dusk , unloaded and sound checked, ate, played and loaded up, and moved out. what else is new? so we didn't get to really see much, and in the context of a stay of a few hours duration it seemed fairly seedy and dangerous. hoods and hookers on the street, although little kids still were playing on the beach. the promoter had his own henchmen; his right hand man was a beat up looking spanish guy, facial scars and an eyepatch; quite an exceptional group of people. the show was in a beautiful old theatre, the best kind of place to play, but there weren't that many people so it felt a little microscopic.

we roll down the highway, davo in the lead—i'm sure THE DEAD are blasting in their van and all is well and high. he's the master of the road and has the perfect methodical demeanor for it. susanne is with martin and mike is with us, keeping everything under control. right now we're cruising off the interstate (how i love to leave it) and down a windy palm and pine rimmed blacktop to the sea.

leaving jacksonville now

leaving jacksonville now. jax bch. this nite was terry's birthday and was incredible. the small club right on the beach, completely grey today, monsoon-like weather with incredibly fierce winds, big grey waves, the beach really smooth and grey/black with sudsy foam scudding along the sands in the wind. most of us had gone out earlier and sat in some very smalltown-type bar to celebrate terry's birthday. it was an incredible place where the clientele are all intimates in some way and are either carousing or fighting with one another. some guy immediately came up to kim with a comment about her boots, and then two women had a brief cat fight, tears and all. we had quite a bit to drink i might add.

on stage, or just prior to it, i had been out with davo smoking, and thurston was sleeping until the moment we took the stage. when he said before white kross "i just woke up" it felt right. it was a set for sleepwalkers—we wound our way as though through uncharted territory, taking liberties at every turn, in confused fusion with purpose. even with the poor p.a. and small stage it was one of those nights where somehow the stars were right; somehow room tone was up high. it was a screaming maelstrom, so much so that during the encore when we were doing "the red and the black" mike and thurston fell backwards into the amps; the whole stack went crashing over backwards in exquisite slo-mo. during the encore it was so loud that i finally couldn't see anymore and for about half the song i stood there with the gtr in front of me, upside down covering my body and my ears, and swinging side to side like some human pendulum. i just couldn't take it.

as for the set, i felt it was one of those special sets that is just out of the norm. sometimes touring gets into a thing which i think we have on this tour, and that's odd for us but it is being able to play the same songs reasonably well every night. last night all that broke apart and it was something different that came out. i felt as though the room was activated, filled with delirious sound. waves of it pushing out as strongly as the gales outside were pushing to get in. the club itself a box being torn by various forces, hovering in mid-air. i think we were all in one state or other from one thing or other. this is pretty convoluted as it's dark as i type thick-fingered on the highway out. we didn't move around much or really make show but some-how it was pretty forceful, in spite of that. we drove some out but a lot just listened, which is the coolest thing. i can't really tell what it would be like to watch our set, sometimes it can be so strange, even to me, that i have no idea what the average viewer sees in it.

PA now and the rivers are running cold, fast and grey. it's beautiful, winter teetering on the edge of the skies. all the leaves are gone and the sky is overcast and low, like it's grazing the roof. it's just great and feels like home, old farm bldgs are collapsing into kindling even as we pass. old dry cornfields. last night i met a girl named kathy b. with the most pure and beautiful blue-gray eyes and looking into them was certainly the highlight of the evening. she said there were many people there on acid, and i would guess that the gig was tailor-made for them—we were slow and everything dripped with molasses, some songs got so hopelessly balled up that it was incredible we continued. some things were actually pretty good, it's just that overall it wasn't the most tight and energetic set. in slo-mo for the acid queens. god!, three days off and we're all soft and out of the routine. i had a kind of fun though, it was one of those strange sets where you don't know what's coming next. the 9:30 was sold out, so there were a lot of folks there to watch us wade thru the cotton candy. the grey-blue eyes were from richmond virginia and i could see that sky through them. pure, driven snow fell on me.

the sky is bright and we head down route 80 to nyc for a gig tonite at irving plaza. last night we played in pottsville—the middle of nowhere, pennsylvania, and it was pretty weird. the hall was real big and the p.a. and lights were real pro but it was an amateur affair otherwise. the kids who came were mostly high school and seemed like they had never seen any shows before. one really funny tall mohawk was trying so hard, these kids were dying to thrash, you could just feel it throughout our (non-thrashable) set. they finally got their chance during "the red and the black" and they revelled in it for those few sweet moments of furious mayhem.

george and terry got pretty wasted and took a room to themselves, looking for jailbait, which was not hard to find. fIREHOSE split after breakfast this morning, mike and davo wanting to hit the city early and go to music stores, but we took the trip over the ridge to Centralia and Mount Carmel, just to see it. we saw some of the locations where the film was shot, and generally grooved on the boondock-backwoods flavor of the place. it's pretty far away, deep into the world. we checked out the coal fires burning under the ground. it was pretty amazing to see these big billowing clouds of smoke coming out of heaps of rubble. it was quite cold out and yet the ground was warm, the rocks hot. some guy who worked for the state stopped to warn us not to climb far onto the piles as they sometimes collapse, taking people or whole bldgs. with them. it hadn't occurred to me previously how insane these fires are—coal ignites somehow underground, and it burns and burns. in centralia it hasn't gone out for twenty years. it's a pretty amazing place, from up on the ridge over town it looked like a matchbox city set amidst the bare trees, houses all boarded up everywhere, smoke billowing up from empty lots all over the town, few cars. just burned out for the most part.

11/26/86

i'm in maryland now, the tour has been over for a few days and it's raining here and almost thanksgiving. like a true novice at the computer i pushed the wrong button and had my last few entries wiped out. here's the jist:

new york was weird. all the people we expected to see were there, and about one thousand others—i hadn't seen so many folks in so long that it was hard to know where to begin. jim and lydia came and i was glad to see them. as for most of the others, i wonder why some of these people keep coming to our shows—they must know what we do by now. i got the feeling somehow of circling vultures.

we had a guitar stolen, which we found out right before showtime, thurston's gibson for expressway, so that made the pre-show scene even more hectic. new york seems to be the place for guitars to be stolen from us. we had to use jay's guitar, which meant he couldn't play kill yr idols with us, and i had to give it the old e#,g tuning in a hurry. we played okay. i think at this point that it's near impossible for us to play one of our great shows in nyc, the pressures are just too weird. i remember going to irving plaza and seeing really cool shows like DNA and the Feelies, Glenn and Laurie Anderson (back then), Gang of Four and Buzzcocks; i thought this was a real concert hall, quite a different type of venue from cb's or max's, a lot more prestigious. but now we're here and it's just another gig to me, no different. I wonder how all these kids see it. i'm so far away from standing in the audience when we play that i have no idea what it must be like.

afterwards the crowd split in a hurry and there was no backstage scene which gave it a slightly sickly-sweet air. fIREHOSE, incidentally, gave it their all and had the crowd going from note one—they must have been really happy about their big show coming off so well—mike was in such a jagged mood beforehand about it.

next show, last show, in amherst with dinosaur and it was great. we played one of our finest, loosest shows in recent days. the sound was great and we just let it out. songs took new turns and shifted with grace. it would be impossible for us to give a show like that in new york somehow, and the difference between these last two nights was just amazing. i often feel that our best shows will always be like this one, in some college dining hall out in the middle of nowhere, standing on tables, away from the green eyes of the big expectant crowds and the press-eaters.

mike hurt his (already fragile) knees at this final show during the starpower part of the encore and was finally persuaded to come out and bear his pain in a chair for "the red and the black." yes, he was the grandfather of punk-rock sitting up there in that chair, surrounded by his cronies and peers. we all shed one final tear as the tour finally faded into the moonless night, and we sacked out in one last motel six, all fairly beat and somehow relieved. suzanne and martin took their own room (finally!). it was more down to the wire for them than any of us. next morning we took off early, not even a farewell breakfast could be held as we were late getting terry to newark for his plane home to texas. fIREHOSE were also going to newark to get watt on a plane home so he could get to a doctor to ease his knee-pain. then the rest of them were going on to ohio to stay at ed's and get some fishing in before taking a long, slow road home. last we saw of them we were drifting apart somewhere near hartford, ct., davo taking the lead to newark.

right NOW is over a week later and new york is back inside me with a vengeance—i can't even remember the tour already, things here have piled up so fast. it's odd the way travels always recede so fast once they're over—as though they were all in a dream, ghostly landscapes drifting over my eyelids, people and places that exist in some far off address of my memory.

—FIN–TELEPATHS JRNL—

27 dec

free at last

free at last, free at last, thank god almighty, i'm free at last. free to lay back and forget about the proper rules of etiquette. free to be a perfect slob and feel at home with the truth. chicago tonight is a cold place in a cold world. i feel the polar night coming on. . . .

jan 1 1987
chicago

dear thom,

hi, hello, how are you? i'm in chicago now and sitting in the late afternoon darkening living room to write you. eighty-seven is here and i'm looking forward to a good good year. these last few weeks of xmas-time have been somewhat of a hell for the most part. I've not felt much in the way of spirit this year, and the scenes at both of our family houses have been less than i'd've liked them to be. that's too bad, too, because as i walk these cold streets here in chicago or down-town oysterbay i know that there is a peaceful feeling to be had that's impossible in nyc where everyone is rushing around in a hurry.

i must say that the two nights you and jeff and i managed to steal away were without a doubt the high points—an affair long forgotten and sorely missed, i hadn't felt such close and needed TALK in a long time, even if we weren't always talking specifically about "something." That wasn't the point, which was, rather, that we COULD talk—about ANYTHING, say anything to each other and find solace and insight there from each other. as i may have said that night, i feel that we are all entering a new stage now, having come from the times we used to talk when the future was wide for all of us, through the times when we each gradually went our own ways to find our lives. now, anyway, we're all in a new place again, similar amongst ourselves in our plights. we're all SOMEWHERE now, and it's time to look up and evaluate exactly where the hell that is. i know that for myself it's meant the revival of much questioning that i hadn't had time for in these last few years of "getting there", but now i see that things must change for me and it's time to reopen the file, to begin asking questions now, because if not now then i'll one day wake up and it'll all be over, i'll not have noticed the time flying by. and let's face it, it goes all too fast as it is without it's going unrecognized to boot.

anyway, tomorrow we leave chicago and return, hopefully, to a few months of peace and industrious work. i'm reading yet another biography of old jacky, called *Desolate Angel*, by Dennis McNally, and it's the very best one i've come across so far. so once again my head is filled with those folks and their times, their visions and hopes.

hope all is well. it's been a long time since i wrote you a real bona-fide lettre, hasn't it?

w love

SIGNS

i'm on the subway and bent into my book, hat pulled brim-down. in my black jacket and workboots i feel that familiar scrutinizing gaze from the rest of the train—they're checking me out, wondering where this character gets off. looking down on me as i sit apart. i imagine it's another place and time and i have a circle on my cap w a black and red swastika emblem. in fact it's burning right up out of my forehead onto the front of my hat, so plugged in am i, it makes me feel so real. WE know what's happening, WE are in touch w the modern world, WE won't be left behind. i feel them all hating me for this which they cannot understand or penetrate. the politics or theory matter not, just that i'm in and they're out. this group is determined, this alliance is a winner. i feel the struggle of the whole of us for the common good. i feel connected to the very roots of the world.

From Here to Infinity
AN ARCHAEOLOGY OF SOUND: 1987

20 jan 87

An Archaeology of Sound

this is a record of a time filled with light and smoke. i purge these sound-shapes from my memory, set them adrift. maybe they will filter in amongst the sediments of yr own memory. maybe a year from now you will hear a sound going around in yr head, as i did. you won't be able to place it. it will stem from somewhere in yr past. you will then own that memory, and we will connect through the force of a sound. SOMETHING, some tones without shape or temporality that have touched me will have touched you. maybe. we will share the experience. that is what history is about, is it not? shared pasts, free from language. images and memories, the coins of the realm. in that time, a year from now, or whenever you hear that sound which you cannot place, then you will know a small part of who i am.

this is a record for everyone w o a turntable. to hang on the wall. the idea of a tape loop, or here a locked groove. "an archaeology of sound" implies that these sound-works have been unearthed, like true artifacts. fractured shards of an object for the listener to complete. one's interaction here determines whether to skip from piece to piece, or let one go round for hours. the final image is assembled in the home.

i don't care about records much anymore, they're somewhat obsolete. i'd rather listen to the trucks roll by my window at night. . . .

13 mar

Thirteen mar
rehearsal is almost over
it's very loud
we're recording a new song
it's not going very well

there are no trees here
i've just found this out
ARTIFACT-INTEL
this is a long day
tomorrow is a long way off

5 april 87

pipeline

stretch me to the point where i stop
run ten thousand miles and then think of me
i think you know the place we should meet
don't worry if it's dark and i'm late

run me out a thin wire
help me to kill this, love
i'll join you tonite at the bottom of the ditch
feel around in the dark until you get the idea

i'm not moving doesn't mean i can't
flame on in my head
my best friend sucked his wife's blood and shriveled up
he was mistaken for sane

we move and groove and cut loose from fear
we'll kill time, we'll shut it down
i've got a pipeline straight to the heart of you
opening in my head

ight glass on a chain being wound around us
he toiling of idle hands
ripping w guilt
a secret form of punishment
axes through skulls
shadow of futility
endless / revolt
the shifting of light and shadows
dividing each existence

no-one is right
nothing is solid
nothing can be held in my hands for long
discontinuity
sandy beaches
rivers sinking into the sea
beautiful confusion
you're a fading memory

we should kill time

**28 april 87
enroute to buffalo from pittsbg**

---

jeff:

i wanted to write you whilst still on tour, before i forget, and tell you about being in Oberlin, which was our third gig of the new material, and the first out of NYC. our first gig in america. right now we're on to buffalo, through rolling hills under beautiful muted chrome clouds. it's been great travelling a bunch in this mid-north-east area—all the river cities and rolling ancient eastern mountain ranges.

this is the old land. so many memories come back, of binghamton and pasts in general. i just wrote thom and was trying to tell him of this vision i had in morgantown, WV the other night, standing out central on a bridge over the big river there. watching the water flow and looking at all the houses stacked up on the hills. trying to figure out where i fit. the houses made no sense to me, i can't see them connected to the world. they're isolated , in a serene vacuum. they seem so finite to me, and so lost in depths. i was made very sad just watching the microcosmic bustle. like some little ant-hill, tiny, on the edge of the whole fucking universe. so small that i was sad for all of our little lives, and tried to wonder how to get out of it, how to eat the world and have it live inside me. how not to feel so cut off. must i always be a traveller of sorts in order to keep a feeling of the world and the larger picture of everything? i couldn't really explain it very well to thom and can't do better here.

but i digress. we played Oberlin, in the Hales gym right on rt. 10 there, it's a nice open hanger space. we had a ten foot green buddha on stage that some of the art students had made for the new gazebo (a travesty of one, actually) across the street. i saw the bldgs. we did an interview at the radio station and saw only a little bit of the place, there wasn't time for more. we had to drive all night on about two hrs sleep, to get there from the nyc gig the night before. we really sucked, everything went wrong from the word go; it was abysmal. i guess we still held a certain amount of focus just trying herculean to combat the ghosts in the machine. we got through, it was so poor, standing there high on an elevated stage with all the house lights on for our set because the pretty colored lights were fucking w our equipment through the electronic matrix. it was like being naked. i fear we didn't fulfill the hopes of the eager oberlin fans who had worked so hard to bring us there. people still seemed to like it, but it wasn't good.

in general, the new stuff is pretty cool, i'll try to get you a tape. my solo gigs start this week, i'm nervous and excited too. don't know what will happen but i feel it to be the start of something good.

we stayed at the holiday inn in Elyria, a place i never heard of before but of which i am sure you know a thing or two about. didn't get to see too much overall but i could somehow imagine you and rob on the streets of this little town. i was looking around, trying w o knowing how, to find your vision of this place; to see it as you two did. reading the street signs and trying to figure out where you walked.

i like the land, there, and through this trip. it's very secure, and comforting; familiar, *familial.*

other than that, things are busy—preparing for trips abroad. it's going to be a busy buncha months from now through october.

met some dead-tape collector last night who gave me a real good tape of 3 mar 87 in oakland. they sound in pretty good form. if the Butthole Surfers come through town you should try and see their acid-media spectacle.

more later,

17 may 87

Project Draft for the Space Gallery, Boston

SCENARIO
A minimum of fifty to seventy-five separate cassette players, each with its own independent speaker unit will be located throughout the space, creating a "field" of sound which will vary with every listening position. Each recorder will be loaded with a tape loop cassette, the whole series of which will be in relationship (i.e. all seventy-five tapes). The nature of this work deals with the specific interaction of these loops, by virtue of their varying proximity and asynchronous loop patterns, the shape of the space, and one's position in the room. All these factors create the final <<music>>.

The space will contain eight to twelve video monitors which will provide the only light. Videotape-loops of vibrating "interference patterns" will be shown, providing an hypnotic visual stimulus. the non-linear nature of these images will further enhance the sensation of time-standing-still. There is no color, just the silver light of flickering black and white patterns.

There will be a haze throughout the space which will be provided by two theatrical smoke-machines, creating a primal, cave-like atmosphere. The space overall should have a fairly rough-hewn appearance, like a basement or abandoned factory.

OVERVIEW

The overall effect would delineate a space of great beauty and impact, where one would be surrounded by a pulsating field of sound and light, the very relationship of which would shift as one moved through the space. Rather than the pristine white room typical of the gallery situation i would create instead a darkened chamber for the mind to explore the repeating cycles of the music. I propose a cathedral of sorts, an environment isolated from the activities of the daily world.

MUSIC VARIATIONS

There would be at least three different cassette tape sequences, each of which would hold quite different musical information (e.g.: pastorale, sustained crescendo, machine-shop interior/rhythmic overlay), which would be installed for alternating periods. The loops will vary in duration from five seconds to thirty minutes.

Variations will include:
- a) a sequence where all cassettes have the same sound source material, playing together but asynchronously, therefore creating a shifting effect through the space.
- b) a sequence including various sound source materials, the spatial interplay more pronounced as one moved through it, more a landscape than the "static field" described in 'a.'
- c) sounds would be shifting from dark, low register to bright high tones, from simple waves to complex rhythm interactions.

DOCUMENTATION

I propose to document this exhibition with the creation of a videotape in lieu of a catalogue. In this manner the sound as well as the image will be available. Such a "catalogue" will consist of two main components: a) shots moving through the space from the spectators point of view, which will include the constant shift in sound texture, and b) images taken from the video loops will be intercut.
A small folder will be included for text and information.

ROOM-TONE AND REPETITION

All music entails very specific interaction with the space in which it is heard. The shape of a room, whether it be a concert hall or one's living room, has a definite affect on the music one hears. This is sometimes termed "room-tone." Under the best circumstances the make-up of the room combines with the sounds being produced, their density and volume, to create something other than just the sum of these elements. Something which borders on the mystical and which can only be spoken of as authentic experience, rather than mere reproduction. Today, when large percentages of one's information are received through secondary sources, as translated data through television or other media, the power of the authentic experience cannot be denied. I would hope to create such an environment as described here, using clusters of repeated tones and textures. Although the power of the repeated tone-sequences is unmistakable, it is also difficult to describe in its hypnotic appeal. I believe its affect stems in part from the sound and rhythm of our own heartbeat—the first music each of us heard.

22 may 1987
en route D.C.—Trenton

r.e.: GUITARS

We just stopped at Chuck Levin's big music store in Maryland and traded in all our old beat up gtr cases for newer (beat up) ones to take to Europe. My Tele-Deluxe case, so beat, yet with me since forever (it still had Jim Wilding's Binghamton phone # masking taped on the edge), was one of those given in trade. I pulled off the metal Fender logo to hang on my wall. That case has toured with me since my first tour with Glenn, housing what will always be my all time favourite guitar. i was trying to trace its lineage:

i bought it during the second FLUKS period in a music store in Endicott, NY. i think it was an even swap for the cream-white tele i had had up till then, and it certainly blew that gtr away, w its double humbuckers and 'f-hole'. Because the varnish had a big scratch through it they swapped me for the cream tele and very little cash, i kept the old case and walked out, unbelieving, w an amazing deal.

Here i am en route from D.C. to Trenton to do one more show and who'd'a thunk that buying that innocent cream white tele (like Geo. Harrison's circa Bangla Desh) and plugging it into a ten-watt Lafayette Radio amp (on '10' in my room upstairs it was simply godlike, then.) would lead down the wire to all this sonic madness.

We've gone through twenty or thirty or more guitars now, yet that tele deluxe is still with me. Just two weeks ago in Morgantown, W. Va. (where the speed limit is already 65 mph!) i found its soul mate—another early '70s tele-deluxe—same humbuckers, same fucking conservative brown wood tone, even the same exact scratch running through the varnish. No 'f-hole' but we bought it anyway and now i have twins.

The escalation continues, we ride the Fender amp/loud/din legacy that Chuck Berry and Duane Eddy and Leo Fender himself all wrought. Soundman, turn me up!

28 may
eindhoven

infinite trip

sitting in an office in the Eindhoven airport (one small bldg).
here's the scenario:

we fly NYC—Gatwick
worry about Infinity suitcase missing the plane
to Maastrict
get assurance it's aboard

fly—Maastrict
it's gone
we lost the tags
we found the tags
they can't find the case
they find it
we panic
·we cool out
it's coming over
we go see Neil and Watt
we stay up late
we go to sleep
we get to airpt
the place is shut
we panic
devise new plan of things to do
we find a way to get to the bag
we go to airpt
the customs man in his weekend clothes
it hasn't come
the flight was cancelled
we can't understand
we panic
we cool out
we cope.

Clean, Out

you move as though everything was still
no movement seem like something to you
if i met you on the street now
walking slow w the radio on
i could look right through you

the images rush over me
deep in the slipstream
feeding this slip'd dream
i jack into *your* matrix
plug into that rush

you're still on the streets
and not moving at all
you stand on the corner
and wait to slip away

reach out a hand
lend me yr hand
don't look///hypnotize
don't look///hypnotize

back to the surface
let me put you back on that street
let me sit you back on that bench there
let me in through yr eyes to raise yr head up slow
stretching yr gaze
past·the cars
down the streets
and off out of bounds

gone, gone by the down shops
and clean out of town.

13 june
a'dam

post-nightmare road

a cloud of smoke still
is filling my eyes.
i'm in the van
steam billowing every everywhere
there is sight
that is no sight
the window is burst screaming trapped
(a screaming eye)
no single thing mattered at that moment

it was over

how close a minute ago had been
Susanne is in the grass pulling off scalding clothes
pale against the green,
beautiful but for the horror of the moment
the peaceful river running down and around as the flash-cars pull up
a simple example of late twentieth-century bridge construction, a barge sixty
years old, ancient in design, drifts down the slide.
the difference between cows roaming fields, small houses tucked into trees, and
the screaming metal hell-in-flames of a moment before.
humanity's reaching arms.
it has been resolved.
get me out.
get me out.

thurs 18 june
paris

it's impossible to believe all the things that have happened since we left the states three weeks or so ago. we have run into such an incredible streak of confusion, bad luck (countered by sonic luck) and weird situations. even trying to recap it all is a monumental task:

even before we left things began to get weird. we found out that our van, which we were trying to sell to dinosaur, is a rattling bucket of bolts about to fall apart, and not the mean lean machine we thought it was. thurston and kim took steve and i, plus terry and vicki, to the airport at newark to fly over for the infinity shows. it seems like ages ago and immediately my mind boggles at the thought. all that last day i had been going wild with final packings and arrangements. dealing with all manner of things and everyone's air flights, i never once thought about our own tickets until we got into the airport.

20 june 87
Zurich

BRICK-RAIN OCCURRENCE

What a dream i had last night. a whole sci-fi novel of a dream, complete w a full cast of characters and a tense alien threat. i could recall it all at the time, in the middle of the night but just couldn't muster the energy to get the notebook and write it down. Now i can remember little of it:

there was a large burned out land area, a cavity or sunken field, an ashen chalky plain. some distance away lay the outskirts of a town. i found myself trudging along through this charred waste when a section of ground not far from me erupted and fell back down as a rain of bricks.

there was a black woman, some sort of street-bum with a camera who kept fig-uring into the plot. in some way the field, which periodically rained down these bricks, was a threat to the town, and i was in the thick of it. the black woman would keep reappearing to snap photos and then either disappear or drop in a faint.

(all this in the corner of my eye)

there was a complete story there, then, in the middle of the night, very scary and very clear to me. i ran over it in my head for memory's sake but come morn it was lost. there's a certain waking post-dream-state logic where things are as clear as still air and yet never visible from a fully lucid consciousness. As though seen clear, but only out of the corner of the eye—look directly and it vanishes. last night was an entire novel, all i'd've had to do was write it down and it would've been done. there was some strong element of fear involved as well. Maybe a new dream jour-nal is in order. often i have these very complete, fully plotted dreams which vanish by morning. some strange shifting of spirits in the mind's eye.

sun 21 june
zurich

thurston and i had to turn around from newark and go back into manhattan to retrieve the tickets, which although insane was a typically sonic start to this long snake of a tour. we arrived the next morning in london and before going on to maastrict we were fairly certain that somehow the suitcase full of infinity gear would get lost. sure enough once arriving in maastrict we located all the guitars and everything but the case. we made an arrangement to have it sent on to the eindhoven airport the next day and were whisked off by carlos first to his house, and then to see neil young in a big hall in rotterdam. from there to utrecht to see fIREHOSE (and bad brains) and commune with watt and davo and gang. by the time we returned to eindhoven to sleep we had all been up for just about thirty or forty hours straight and sunk into complete euro-oblivion.

zurich is a town whose church bells never stop ringing. their echo is always in the streets, waiting just for me.

22 june
turino

We're in italy now, it's the first summer we've hit, left all the rain behind the alps, and it feels real good to be here. In contrast to our expectations of thieves and confusion we've found instead everything to be very relaxed and warm, wonderful and secure. This place is at the moment like a haven for me, some sort of solace amidst the great distances. I feel a certain sense of release here. An easing up of the general tensions and strain.

fri 26 june
munchen

what a day this was. i awoke in a terrible cloudy mood in ljubijana, had a breakfast which consisted of some sort of chocolate spread on a roll, a burst of sugar at the time but which later proved to be a knot of lead pipe in my system, making a terrible mood even worse. we had a long drive to munich today, leaving behind the sun of italy for the european rain (again). i'm bored right now and my mind is in another place. these drives, through incredible castle-ridden country, have not really been very inspirational to me. there seems to be a wall up right now, a block of some sort which has my mind preoccupied with other places and things.

we split up from the van late in the day because it is much slower than the car and i wanted to get the feel of the autobahn at 100 miles per. after getting slightly lost in the city traffic we arrived at the venue to find the van already there, it having pulled up shortly before us somehow, and all these germans screaming because we were late. so late in fact that the Lounge Lizards were going to play without us at all on the bill (and what a stupid bill to begin with but that's another story).

the promoter, a german egoist asshole named roger, wouldn't let us play, even though the equipment was inside and we had agreed to forego soundcheck. we had worked with roger before on past tours and somehow something had always gone awry. the last time we played for him we were *many* hours late, and now he was ready to even the score.

a long winded fight ensued as only the germans know how to stage. we ended up in front of the crowd, thurston and me on top of the van playing "master-dik" out of the blaster, him blowing his police whistle and me announcing the whole fiasco to the crowd waiting to get in, just to keep the record straight and cause some ruckus. we played some rap tapes and sold tee shirts and posters in the parking lot, talking to some disappointed people who'd actually come to see us. out of the crowd pops ken friedman and adrian, here promoting *Made in USA* at the munich filmfest. how weird to see them there. so after all the fuss was over we went back into town, along with jochen who was along as jeanette's (evil jeanette) representative. we all went out to eat and had some general social fun for a few hours in the midst of another snag in this snaggly tooth of a tour. it sure was more fun than doing a gig. so we sat, displaced new yorkers, hollywoodians, and a dutchman, eating italian food in bavaria.

Euro-Infinity Journals: 1987

it seems impossible to account for all the lapses in concentration and all the stupid situations that have gone down on this tour of jinx and hijinks. that second morning in holland we woke up with a fair assurance that the infinity suitcase should have arrived into eindhoven airport about an hour or two before we awoke. going to the airport however we found it to be completely closed for some dutch holiday. still bleary and now quite perplexed we returned to carlos' house to plan for the first gig that night. we began making some new tapes for the show. later that afternoon a glimmer of hope came as ton van gool was able to get the airport opened up for us and a customs man was there at the otherwise deserted terminal to help us find the bag. "this is it, i thought, we're saved!" but somehow the bag was not there anyway. we found that the plane had been canceled and never made the trip to begin with. ho hum. we, or rather i, was getting pretty desperate at this point. we went to the club and worked something out, found a mixer, made some tapes and decided to play live a bit. i set up four amps and we had a drum kit. after mixing tapes for a short while we shifted into a playing mode, with steve going beat-wild on the drums and me setting all four amps to feeding back until a loud (natch) beating din was established which we then played off of for awhile. it actually turned out to be a very cool and new show, forcing the live playing into the act which i had wanted anyway. we crashed late again, the jet lag beginning to get to us now.

next day same thing at the airport, which was open but again the plane had been cancelled. i spent most of this day on the phone to stupid baggage porters at gatwick trying to sort the mess out. there's just no accounting for the english mind. it seems the suitcase had richard brewster's name and address on it which i had forgotten to remove and which caused further confusion. arrangements were finally made to have it sent that night to amsterdam where steve and i could pick it up for the show in den haag, not too far away. oddly enough, it actually *was* waiting for us when we got there, and we drove back to the club in den haag, planning to incorporate the live and the tape stuff. i'd been reading some new things i'd written the day before on carlos' 'typowriter' in between pacing and pondering that first night's show. the set opened with this beat box mix of thurston scratching a hendrix record along to a drum track which we had made at martin's during the "master-dik" remix a week or so before. i would read the piece about julie and the boat over top of that. that was working out pretty cool. a good, somewhat perplexing way to open the set. this nights' gig was marred by a feedback squeal during the live part which broke the momentum and generally fucked things up. plus the den haag crowd, notorious for being about as lively as tombstones, were no help. fIREHOSE were on the bill and they didn't fare much better with the crowd, although it was cool that we and they were both there, in holland, like, you know, together.

next day we were off to the little town of Goes among the dikes of zeeland, the southern-most part of holland where we'd never been before, up against the atlantic. this is the area of the great and devastating flood of the 1950's, before the modern dikes were built. we tried to see the dykes, huge and great feats of modern engineering technology, but they were fenced off from the public.

ACCIDENT
now comes the next installment in what at that point couldn't yet be seen as one in a long list of crazy happenstances. we're driving along. carlos and vicki in carlos' brand new red peugeot, and me, steve and terry in our small infinity wagon behind. stopped at an intersection, carlos is both reading the map and pulling out onto the hiway, when a car whizzing along, surprised to find that carlos doesn't see him at all, sideswipes them, ripping the whole front end of carlos' car to shreds and mangling one entire side of their own car. it all happened so fast, just a screech and low thwap of metal to metal as they impacted. no-one was hurt thankfully and we spent an hour or two getting things straight with the other folks and the cops (it was c's fault), waiting amongst fields of cows for the towtruck to come to carry the poor peugeot home to eindhoven for cosmetic and structural surgery. carlos was fairly bummed out and mad at himself and he related to us the story of how he had pulled the very same stunt a few years ago, resulting in an almost identical accident.

THE SHOW
the show in Goes was pretty cool, it kind of found its shape: hendrix tape plus read-ing the julie piece, tape mixing section, droning amps rising, drums entering//live

playing section, and out with final tape mixing and bells. the video screens looked okay onstage. i think it proved to be kind of nice and confusing, a bit involving and a bit aloof, generally quite unlike anything the audience was prepared to see, which is fine by me. also on the bill was World Domination Party who were pretty cool and nice guys to boot. turns out they're on rob collins' products inc. label at mute. kind of noise/blues, with a good style. i think they've listened to their fair share of neo-ameri-wave *(e.g.: us 'n' stuff)*.

the final show for us the next day was in paradiso, amsterdam. rather than the giant room where there were already four bands to go on, we had a smaller room upstairs all to ourselves, we were able to do a nice long check and position the three TV's nicely on top of the pa speakers and one onstage which made for a nice three-dimensional synapse-snap view of the video-feedback scans, davo told me later. the show was the best yet and the room was jammed with all manner of folk including daniel miller and rob collins and the three Ut girls whom i hung with afterwards but while it was happening i was oblivious to all of them, really inside the sounds and the reflected glare of the vid-screens. for the second reading, while steve wailed beat-rain over me i was crouched in front of the screen onstage, trying to enter it, silhouetted in the electron glow. it felt really good and the crowd seemed really to like it.

fIREHOSE were also on the bill, last in the big room and although they had a bit of a hard time and lots of folks had burned out and left by then, they still went over pretty well with those who stayed. i wasn't to see a show by them that felt comfortable (for them, to me) until some days later in england. it was good to have those guys around though, with davo on the case, a true master of space and time, and mike with a monkey wrench shooting off in twenty hyperbolic directions at once, drooling and gibbering like the end of the world was at hand, ed being cool with his U2 bootleg outtakes from the joshua tree, and george relaxed and semi-perplexed at all the fuss, drumsticks in his sock, blue eyes taking it all in *and* scouting for chicks.

that's holland for the infinity tour, maybe the one and only. we left the next noon from amsterdam to london via plane, coming through customs about twenty minutes before kim, thurston and suzanne arrived from the states. they were supposed to have been in already but were delayed for hours at newark. suddenly we found ourselves in a little quarantine room greeting each other while the customs people reviewed our latest working papers scam. we got in, found paul, i hefted the video camera to record for posterity the famous arrival, and england had begun.

* * *

the u.k. was a mixture of rain, fuckups, absurd anglo-isms, renewed acquaintances, triumphs, and can't-wait-to-leave-here's. we settled in richard boon's, jo and pinko's, and pat's, had some good beer, and planned the week out. spent some time at the mute office checking out the sister merchandise (tee shirts, huge and beautiful posters, the record itself and my record too, at last—on clear instead of gray vinyl), saw mick harvey and some others, checked out the new big black record sleeve, hung out.

next day was interviews and photos all day at the offices, just an interminable string of them. it was lucky that they went in descending order of import, because we all wearied after the first few. the most interesting was with the 'legendary stud brothers' from melody maker whom paul had a complete suspicion and distrust of even prior to their arrival. they tried to get all socio-political on us, one of them asking all the questions and the other doing the silent bit. we filmed them with the video camera and generally deflected the stupid questions while at the same time having some engaging moments of conversation.

interviews have been weird all along this tour. people refuse to believe we don't have some big new statement to make, or that it's really all encapsulated in the music. they want from us what it is we're "into" now, what's our concept; they refuse to believe when we say we're still just doing what we do, trying hard and making songs. there's all this about sister being evol II and everyone is so ready to be able to peg us in a slot and set us adrift. "ah so that's SY! now we've got them," stupid critic-think.

we followed one of the studs into the bathroom with the video when he had to pee and that seemed to really disturb him, which we found funny. he kept saying "this isn't fair," while i shot away and thurston narrated: "this is the famous and legendary stud brother having a whizz in the mute stalls!"

we did a photo session with some guy along the canal behind mute which seemed really stupid at the time but which looked really good two weeks later in the *NME*. the best photo session was with peter anderson, a scottish guy working for *sounds,* in his loft the next day where in a large white room he'd drawn a big red spiral on the wall in spray paint for us to float and anti-grav in front of.

that night we saw the infamous van which was to plague us for the coming weeks, a huge white iveco with airplane seats and video, tee vee, stereo, larger than anything we'd ever travelled in before. noel was to be the driver so at least we wouldn't have to deal with that situation until europe a week later. we threw the guitars in and split.

the next day we had to be up somewhat early for rehearsal in some fancy rehearsal studio. we got there all bleary, earlier than we'd really wanted to get up, and upon arrival found out that the van with equipment and guitars hadn't yet arrived. paul was phoning like mad on the portable phone he had for the weeks of the tour (which was quite a cool thing to have i must say—it's the futcha). it finally turned out that the van had a flat and the wheel was so frozen on that it couldn't be removed, so we had to wait while a second, temporary van was rented, loaded up and brought over to the place.

when they finally did turn up terry, noel and some sleazy third guy who was to plague us for the next few days (with a sleazy, greasy little upper lip fuzz and all), they were completely beaten and exhausted from the mornings' problems. it turned a three-hour rehearsal into an all day affair. the amps were fucked and inadequate and someone from the equipment rental company came in a van with ten other amps for us to try. we found one really cool music man and then they went away and some time later brought us another one just like it, so that seemed cool. we stumbled through the rehearsal with the bad amps meanwhile, hideous sounding and fIREHOSE had just arrived and were listening to this squall, mike immediately off and raving as we tried to rehearse.

trying to pad the set a bit we tried to rehearse "green light" and "marilyn moore," neither of which got off the ground, and ended up trying "i wanna be yr dog" for the first time in years, which was alright. now the fun begins: it turns out that iggy himself is down the hall whipping and strutting his euro tour band into shape (w barry adamson amongst them), and we see him in the hall. kim peeks into his rehearsal while *they're* doing "dog" in order to see what the third verse is. later we all meet him and pay respects which is so cool even now, in a kind of a cartoon-ceremonial way, and he asks to come see us tomorrow so we say well, yeah, we suppose we can manage to squeeze him onto the list. we leave in a state of utter cool vibes, laughing and whooping, give him a *sister* tee shirt and are off into the london night to a party in our honor, being thrown at doug (from mary chain)'s club, where fIREHOSE will play for our entertainment.

it's a big fuckin' jammed event, super crowded, smoke-filled and fairly unbearable, but everyone is there and it's good to see them but too absurd to try to talk to them in the crowd and the din. it's an okay time but a bit over the top. finally late, very late in the evening, we are released to go home. steve and vicki and i along w jo and pinko go to their place. i'm leaving the talk about the coke snow-storms and the hash out of all this because it's basically uninteresting stuff: who was high on what, or how many people were crammed into the men's room trying to get iver to cut them a line, or who had the acid in their matchbox. it all went down, and i was caught in the flurries when possible, i admit it, but what else was there to do to break the monotony and feel the razor's edge? that shit's all beside the point. we have no infatuation with that stuff, just a giggle as the fabs would have said.

speaking of whom, it was on june first 'twenty years ago today' and everyone and everything is pepper-mad and the cd is out and all are celebrating. it still stands to me as a great record, the production and conceptualization especially. a few years ago i had thought it sounded really dated but listening again last week on the headphones i didn't find that at all, just mainly good songs. just yesterday paul informed us that there's to be a big charity remake of sgt pepper's and it's to include elvis costello and all these big wigs and we have been asked to be included, the smallest band to be invited. also among the news yesterday was the report that we are to receive a gold record for the version of "white kross" which was on that last NME give-away 7" a few months ago. seems it sold unusually well . . . . perfect for that bathroom wall . . . .

30 june
bielefeld

what a weird and splendid show tonight in spite of everything. my amp blew both speakers half way thru and i ended up using a big marshal stack of gore's, which was weird , but it was a really good, concentrated set. the sound was good and we hit some cool passages. lately the music has been really opening up, it's really music again, after a week of doldrums which followed the first wave of getting good at playing the songs, now we're playing the set, whole. it's such a great rush when onstage and everything is all heading right down the pipe and hitting some sort of collective bullseye. tonight was full of starts and stops, but the people stayed with it. at one point a stretched out ending got real quiet for awhile before it was over; after we stopped playing there was absolute silence in the hall, with at least a couple of hundred people standing there just staring, not talking a word for over a minute. it was great.

today was cody's second birthday, and i spoke to him tonight on the phone for some minutes. he stuck with it this time, he's not too clear on the phone thing yet. it was great to speak to him and have him reply. two years of little life. amazing and wonderful. . . .

thurs 2 july
berlin

we played in berlin tonight, the worst gig we've done here in years, ever, probably. it's been a long night of meeting and greeting in the dressing room, monica kid congo chris bohn some crazed americans, kenny and adrian again, and then out to eat. late night *imbiss* with kenny and some strange nyc rock chick he'd picked up at the gig and mick harvey and friends and adrian and his perfect pale skinned rainbow. it was one of those interminable and awkward evenings.

something i realized though at the end of this evening: the band is really good and the people are all fine and sane. we argue and get all pent up on the road and everyone is grumpy and no-one gets what they want often enough but that's beside the point. after all this time we've got a system down, however imperfect, with which to deal with all the stress, and what we do together is stronger than all the folly and personal differences. it's something very good, and big, and somehow very right.

3 july
hamburg

The Postcard Inside Me

still in the hotel, doors slamming, people screaming—a crazy fucking european nightmare of arguments and deals and brainwashed flunkies doing the bidding and story after lie after lie after story. dark night plotting business money crap crying hysterical petty can i write you a check not to cash for two weeks bullshit. wake up we're here!

what did i see?
i saw a town as big as a postcard. there was a landscape the size of a stamp. i'm not sure what i saw there. i remembered drawings—big and black w charcoal, and straight and beautiful lines. with all the space in the world drawn in dark black love. deep. there were photographs of people in groups, and cars parked by the tiny roads. reflecting light from a picture to a drawing to a landscape. somehow all of hamburg tonight was a great overworked drawing by that spanish painter with the beautiful name i can't remember... lines scratched in, etched, and then scrubbed out, erased, redrawn until every shape locked into place. it stood before me just like that, etched in a copper plate. a tiny toy of a town. i knew every detail, looking out over the train station platform, or down upon the fading image of the

tracks coming up over the land from the horizon in hard brown steel behind the Markt Halle. i was alone inside the postcard.

5 july
roskilde

NONE OF YOU CAN TOUCH ME NOW. MY MIND IS SEALED LIKE A CRYPT. IT IS SILENT AND STILL ON THE CURVE OF THIS FRAGILE EARTH. THE SUN DOING ITS BRIGHT SILVER SWORDS-OF-SATELLITES DANCE ACROSS THE WATER. CLIMBING THE GREEN TO ME. BINARY FLASH FIGURES ROOTING FOR THE MOON LIKE THE SILICON MATRIX GONE HAYWIRE. ON AND OFF, ON, OFF AGAIN. ENDLESSLY REPEATING. I SEE A PICTURE OF ONE BEAUTIFUL WOMAN HIDDEN AMONGST THE BURNING FLARES. MUTATING. CHANGING. FLICKER-ING IN AND OUT OF VIEW. THE SUN GOES DOWN AND HER FACE TURNS PALLID GOLD AND THEN ROSE BLUE. SO BEAUTIFUL ABOUT THE MOON.

NONE OF YOU ENTER HERE ANYMORE. IN THE CHAMBER OF MY SILENT THOUGHTS OF NOTHING I AM FREE. I DONT CARE ABOUT YR PETTY DESIRES, ABOUT HOW YR BORED OR HAVE SCUFFED YR SHOES. MY SHOES ARE TIED IN KNOTS FROM THE WEAR AND TEAR. I DONT UNDERSTAND WHAT YOUR PROBLEMS ARE. YOU SPEAK OF FRIENDSHIP, I CAN ONLY SEE A VACANCY. YR EYES LIKE TWO USED CAR LOTS, NOT A SERVICEABLE THOUGHT IN THE YARD.

INVENT, GO INVENT A MACHINE TO THINK UP YR THOUGHTS FOR YOU. AT LEAST THEN YOU'LL HAVE SOME TO PASS OUT AT PARTIES AND AMUSE YR PETS. ME I DONT NEED NOT ONE THOUGHT AT THIS MOMENT. I DONT NEED TO BE, OR TO GUIDE YOU. I CAN SEE THE GOLDEN SURFACE BREAKING APART. AS PLAIN AS THE FACE IN MY HANDS.

I KNOW WHICH WAY THE SKY FALLS WHEN IT'S TIME FOR THE SUN TO GO DOWN. I CANT HEAR YR VOICES THRU THE SOUNDS OF THE BIRDS MADLY

CACKLING IN THE REEDS OFFSHORE, AND THIS FLOCK OF HELICOPTERS BEATING TIME OVERHEAD. STIRRING UP THE SURFACE OF THE LAKE, DISSOLVING THE SUNLIGHT IN A SHIMMER OF GOLDEN HUES. OH CLAUDE MONET SHOULD BE HERE NOW! HE INVENTED THIS PICTURE, DIDN'T HE? HE TOLD ME ALL ABOUT IT, THE PALE COLORS IN BEAUTIFUL INTERCOURSE.

SUDDENLY I SEE WHAT I'VE GOT. AMIDST A SEA OF STONES I'VE FOUND A FISH! WITHOUT A BONE. I TOSS IT BACK TO RUB STONE ON STONE. I'LL BE GONE WHEN THE SUN FADES BEHIND THE HILL. THOUGHTS OF YOU WILL BE GONE LONG BEFORE THAT. BURNING QUIETLY. SMOLDERING TO ASH IN THIS DUSKY STILLNESS. YOU AND YR POOR THOUGHTS OF DESIRE AND BETRAY-AL. MY PEN MOURNS THE PASSING OF YOUR HUMANITY AND THE LOSS OF SACRIFICE. THESE WORDS, CRUCIFIED BY THEIR OWN ACTIONS, LAUGH NOW TO SEE YOU STARING BLINDLY W YR MOUTHS OPEN, TRYING TO BUY UP W YR WALLET ALL THE INSIGHT YOU'D LIKE TO HAVE IN THIS LIFE. TRYING TO OWN THE IDEAS THAT STRIKE YR FANCY.

YOU CAN'T HOLD IDEAS, THEY PASS THRU YOUR HANDS AS IF THRU AN OLD RUSTY BUCKET SPLIT AT THE SEAMS. I KNOW WHAT I SEE IN THE MIRROR. I DONT NEED YOU FOR A PARANOID REFLECTION. NO CONSUMER HERO, NO MAKER OF ROADS, NO SILENT SENTINEL. ALL THE LISTS ARE CRUSHED FOR-EVER. ALL OF THIS WILL GO ON w O YR TINY MINDS TO INTERFERE.

I'M JUST GOING TO WAIT HERE, TILL THE SUN SETS, THE LIGHT LIFTS AND I'M FINALLY FREE, AND CLEAR. THE BEADS OF GLASS, THE GOLDEN LIGHTS, GROW SMALLER STILL, MORE FRACTURED, LESS DISTINCT, PART OF THE INFINITE GLOWING.

9 july
Stockholm

here we are in the red light district of stockholm, almost done. street filled with junkies and tourists, a unique and volatile combination. due to a twenty-four-hour period of utmost depression a few days ago, during and after the giant roskilde fest, i had decided to give up this journal, wanted to pack in *everything* and fucking give up. those periods are good in retrospect, but at the time everything and everyone was a drag. now i'm over that for better or worse—sometimes the thought of giving all this mindfuck up is very sensible; it's not an idle desire. the thing is, all this craziness is both a stimulation for the mind, and something which drives you insane, with all the schedules and people to be pleased and included on things, it's not an easy way to exist and keep abreast, keep moving forward. it's a moving, hurried *stasis*, sometimes.

the last gig on the continent is through, but we've still got three weeks here to go. it's seems like forever, both behind and ahead. scandinavia was both an infatuation and a bore, simultaneously. it's a strange place. it's now after midnight here and the sky is still a dark milk-blue. at any time of day the bulbs of cloud are massing in strange heraldic patterns of light and dark, steel blues through all blues into pinks and yellows, always dramatic like old oil paintings. it gets late but never dark. the sky is a constant visual phenomenon at this time of year; it doesn't go home at night. very cool.

tomorrow we head back to fucking england.

tue 14 july
london

finished the first day at southern studios. things went well and i began to wish we had a month to record right now instead of just a few days. john loder is a great and funny fellow to be working with, he works really fast and things sound really good. he has these huge speakers that he kept flicking on at maximum volume without warning. the four of us found ourselves flattened against the back wall of the control room. maybe we'll do the ciccone valentine's lp here in november. yesterday we planned the next year, sitting over at mute in a summer snowstorm w paul and carlos, and it's one of the things on the list.

the gig of the night before last was a great final blowout, so loud and crowded with people jamming in, spilling out onto the street. we played great; with a screaming crowd from the word go pressed against the stage. it's a good bet for a good gig. These Immortal Souls, rowland and epic's new band opened, their first gig, they were real good.

what about the rest of the tour story? the exploding van, the munich fiasco, italy, hüsker dü, the tivoli, jeanette, my black mood of denmark, all the lost roads we travelled. . . . the computer is out of memory and i need to dump all this quick so i can stream all the rest of it before we turn for home, less than 2 weeks away now. more story left to tell. . . .

18 july
woodgreen, london

DEATHTRIP

thought i could've died of a heart attack last night—whole body filled w aches and stresses and pains of various sorts. Heart racing, p'raps from the coke; i guess so. couldn't fall asleep, pains kept waking me and i felt as though those could've been my last moments of life. what a terrible thing to feel, so far from home and in such a wasted situation, so far away. . . . the blood was rushing, pulsation through me felt as though my fingertips would pop off and blood would be running everywhere. the pressure was intense in my neck and limbs. isn't that the sign of imminent heart failure? this week these thoughts of death have been popping up, seeing Big Black's *sound of impact* record, about the final moments of all these airplanes before crash. what a hideous way to go. death is a major fear for me—to think i'll go before i'll really have done anything, it's about the most hideous thing imaginable. just have to make it thru one more week, and then we'll be home together. i can't wait.

one more day in england, tomorrow we leave and that's fine by me, it's a horrible country and i despise it more and more, the more i'm here. something very unhealthy about it here. i always get sick when we're here. sick to death.

last night i kept startling awake, right on the verge of sleep, feeling as though i'd be gone forever if i lost consciousness—just waiting for morning light to come. is it just the drugs? sending my system into convulsions? my body is frail, chest caving in, and i mistreat it, abuse it. it's easy to fall into. what would cody think to know i'm slowly killing myself off from his life? killing his father?

this unsettled life, which can be so inspirational, is just a drag now, a wait i must endure, hazards i must hurdle before going home.

(and summer's almost gone).

21 july
belgium

i'm sitting on the edge of the stage at Pukkelpop, Big Black is 10′ from me and the crowd is, in part, in a manic belgian circle dance right now. the sound is good. we're on next. it's the last show of the tour. my body feels vague and fragile. i'm not high in any way; my heart is a fragile vessel right now. we'll get up in a short while and rock out. the crowd wants us lost, they want to see us flail and writhe, act out their own aggressions. as i said i'm straight now and glad, and that makes it a harder thing to get lost in the music and really forget, go wild. but i want to get lost today on stage, come out and play and feel the blood flow through my veins, cease the pounding needle pains in my head which have been a plague of late. the electricity should heal me and burn out the sys-fog i've been experiencing. peace frog. big black a muscle of squeal-attack and fast gliding electric waves. we're up next.

the more i feel healthy, the more i feel weak. the more i feel sick, the more i feel better. we're up next and i'm straight ahead cold standin' on the turf. time to get lost.

21 july
bruxelles

the last gig is over and i've a bit of time to myself in the hotel tonight. two more days in holland and we're off for home. i saw a beautiful woman today at the festival and we had a relationship through gazes, from the stage area while Wire were on. what wonderful eyes and a wonderful face. it was quite amazing because without saying a word to each other or touching or being in a very close proximity we had quite a full relationship just through the eyes. so satisfying. it was very beautiful and delicate and complete in itself, a blown kiss from her and it was over. no names, no games, just a tunnel of desires flowing between us that said it all, what was and what could have been. it didn't have to be. it was already complete.

23 july
hilversum, NL

tomorrow we leave for new york—two months to the day since steve and i arrived. things are almost wound up now, the days in holland are warm with a beautiful cool breeze, birds singing and generally very summer-peace-full. in the room across the hall strains of a "Kotton Krown" mix filter dully through. it sounds great with the wind blowing through this window. we're spending so much time in studios all over the place these days; what was once a seemingly impossible dream is now a sort of pedestrian reality. it's good though, we haven't yet figured out how, really, to mix records, but we get better at it bit by bit. it's a wonderful headache of a job.

i had to go to a doctor here today to see about this liquid filing my ears. it turns out they are infected and i now have to take penicillin for awhile. we've got to leave here soon to go back to carlos' to pack. the wind is in my face and its very touch feels like the best poetry. so soft and evocative of every summer wind that's ever been.

this was a weird two months. no real visions came on this tour, lots of events were absorbed along the way instead. it was not a romantic hallucinogenic visionary time, much drier and more sedate than that. there were so many factors constantly to consider. i think we're moving into a different phase w the touring now. some of the more pleasant aspects, the sights and cities, are being lost under the work load. we're definitely on our way towards a new phase, whatever it may be.

tomorrow everything is going to rapidly shift gears, like stepping off a moving sidewalk. all the supposed freedom of being on tour, the independence and power of movement, will be reigned in. yet it won't be replaced by a peaceful stretch of creative solitude, but rather by a few short and hectic weeks before the next tour. we'll see what happens next.

GREETINGS FROM NOWHERE

hello good buddy
do you ever contemplate writing a letter and go over in yr mind all the topics
which you'll cover and the way in which you'll describe things? and then find upon
writing that about half those things get restated and the other half lost forever?
well, i do all the time and the letters in my head are sometimes much better than
the ones which get sent. misfortune. i already wrote you this one in that manner
and it was quite good and said all i had on my mind, but now i must try again and
begin at the start.

we're in chicago now and it's almost midweek. it's about as mellow an evening
as summer can provide, a fine cool breeze, no moon, crickets and darkness
broken by the sound of an occasional suburban car gliding by. i'm in a rare mood
of reflection and i'm not quite sure what. a mixture of melancholy and out and out
sadness and a few other emotions all at once. we stay here another few days and
then head for the blue ridge mts. right now all is quiet, cody is asleep and amanda
is watching tv with her folks in the next room.

i've been reading the most wonderful book, hemingway's "latest," *The Garden
Of Eden,* which came out within the last year. especially great in the spirit of
romantic vacations and artists working and making love by the sea, in france and
spain. w cool wines and freshly pressed clothes. it's a fantastic book which i will
loan you, among his very best. it deals with sex in a more frank manner than he'd
done before. very sad and romantic, yet strong, written at the end of his life when
he found fault w everything. i'm some four chapters from the end now and i just
had to put it down for awhile. i don't want it to be over just yet. it's too beautiful.
the writer is strong and certain in his work and watches his marriage convolute
into a menage a trois, distort, crumble, reshape, become totally out of control. his
life is uncontrollable, while in his work he remains constant. i've always envied the
image of the artist who could travel and work anywhere while maintaining a full
and romantic social life as well. it's a great book and perfect for this moment.

i'm at a loss to see myself and my life clearly at the moment, except to know that something is amiss and that i don't feel in the least in control. my decision-making power has atrophied somewhere along the way. no feeling of control or real personal and individual fulfillment, in spite of all the success, within which i can clearly see my part. "the future's uncertain and the end is always near" a wise man said.

i saw james that nite in NYC and he's busily climbing the ladder and saying "go for the cash" and "you're 31, lee," and "put yr money in australian gold mines" and "when the next depression hits how prepared will you be?" it's all causing my head to spin. jeff's gonna be a doctor and rob is what he is and i see everyone settled down and somewhat satisfied, having made the big choices, and i still haven't.

i have no certain future, no money to purchase our dream house now or in any foreseeable future, no superb artistic vision at the moment. in short right now it feels i have very little indeed. where will i be in five years? my head swims. i made a painting yesterday, my first from life in six or seven years and it's a terrible little painting. i don't know what else i could've expected but it left me very hurt and with the knowledge of how much time and concentration i've lost in that area and how much i need to regain. so i have no true art fulfillment, and no financial security. very little indeed, buddy. i feel revolted by the whole thing at times and sometimes i wish i was twenty-five again and single and could go bury my fucking head somewhere w no son to be responsible for and no "reputation" to live up to.

the way i figure it right now there'll never be a beautiful house full of all the great furniture and design i see in magazines on an amazing parcel of land with a small stream and big trees and a porch swing and footbridge and maybe a horse and a mountain and a good car and studio barn and a fireplace w candlesticks and air-tix to the summer spot in spain waiting on the dresser. calm society and peer respect and leisure and ART and fulfillment and whatnotallelse. it'll just never happen as far as i can see.

i'm not sure of anything right now and i don't want it to go away. i want it to stay until i resolve it once and for all. i've found myself wondering if maybe the trade-off of some job for the money to lead a life w all of the above included isn't really a better answer than i'd thought it was. w a pension, etc. look at david, all his life spent working and when can he retire or ease up and on what? never, w nothing saved and mainly making shit for shitheads his whole life besides. and then see james (who is a dear friend in spite of his use as an example here) coasting along, teaching classes stoned and going to live in firenze to teach for a term and already making 36G a year not to mention his girlfriend's salary and how easy it seems and how neatly pressed his clothes are. why is it so easy for some to have everything they want w no sweat at all and so difficult for others to have anything at all, and have to try so hard besides?

i sometimes think i'm trying too hard for too little, and taking life too serious and with too much of a capital L instead of pouring another drink and sitting back and waiting somehow to slip through the cracks to the top. our lives seem so small in scope. we'll never be president or climb beyond our own little rooms. sometimes it seems hopeless from here on out, no matter what kind of security may come.

well anyway that's it and most of the first letter in my head came out here and now i've gotten some of it off my chest which doesn't make it any easier but not harder either. i'm going to go finish that book now so its greatness won't hang over me and further color my days. will return around 25 august or so, see you then. write me a reply will you, no matter how brief or extensive, so i have one true letter lying in my box among the business mail when i return.

thanx.

2 oct 87
oregon

[PHIL]   we were driving along route 101 in northern california. it was late at night, we still hadn't made much time up from san francisco. giant trees were looming out of the darkness on either side of the car, these fabulously large and gray shapes rising up on either side of the road; living sentinels as we drove past in our tiny travels. no one was talking, the trees were moving past, gliding almost, and I felt very alone with them. i got to thinking about the lonely darkness we were driving thru, too hurried on our stupid and purposeful way to even get out of the car and stand among these huge beings of time.

we were driving along and somehow Lordes was in my head. how did I come to be thinking of her? we had passed a metal-frame bridge, very like the one on s. washington is binghamton, same fading green/gray paint, but i don't think that was it. how did it happen? somehow the landscape rushing past had something to do with it (and i told myself i was going to forget the landscape). i remember her even now, so much later. I wonder where she is. last I heard, years ago, she was in san francisco, using her body to support herself. what an easy way out for her. could she still remember me? i wonder if memories link us in a complete connection, or does she now exist in my head alone? in the museum of my memory...

she'll always be linked with a certain period of my life, bound up with certain ideas and feelings. my life then wasnt only faces and locations, there were feelings then that i've not felt since, emotions and ideas frozen along with the time and place.

she was small, and dark, a jewish girl from brooklyn clinging to her beauty; her sexuality her only hope. came from a crazy fucked-up family, plenty of money around to spoil her and by 16 make her immune to the material side of life, because she really had never needed to buy into it, you see. she'd had the ballet lessons and everything she wanted, she was spoiled beyond saturation, into a delicate hate. jaded, she had to have money, never dreamed she might ever be without it, left to fend for herself. that came later, willfully, a stab at maturity, at growing up/crossing the line she could never cross. money was always sent to her. her parents neurotic, fucked up, divorced, her dizzy mother raising dogs with some boy friend and going off the deep end, lost in space, a scary mirror—reflection of what might lay ahead. an older sister, whom I always imagined as a duplicate of Lordes's dark beauty, somewhere. she was young, 16 i think in freshman year, and already an artist. the first true one i'd met in my life. she could paint from life and draw crazy mystical psychosexual drawings that poured out with a natural, unselfconscious ease. beautiful figures sculpted with a pencil point, entwining, embracing, orgies of them like some roman frieze. she could do the same with words, writing sophisticated and very hip babble loaded with frank sexuality unconcealed. she would sleep with anyone that caught her fancy. used it I suppose as a way of knowing people and being held. She was lonely inside and needed to be wanted.

never had i previously been so enraptured of a person as I was of her. I wanted her so much, mentally as well as physically—and was at the same time frightened by the demonic ease, the cold cruel honesty with which she seemed to move through her days. she had a spark and carried it freely. she could deduce the truth in any situation and get away with it, do you know what I mean? we went through a lot together, getting close but not physical. we didn't always understand each other, we grew up in such different worlds, only 40 miles apart! I would watch along with everyone else while she had one beautiful boy after the next. I couldn't understand her attraction to these dopes who were merely gorgeous.

here i was smart and trying to deny it almost, yet quite self-conscious where sex was concerned. she was smart, yet naturally physical as well, able retreat within herself, floating above the surface of the relationships she was having. something i'd never want to do, but she lived at a remove, trying to free herself of life's binds. she was into ram dass, be here now, and every religious fad touched her in some way. she was trying to escape to India, really trying to understand the concepts there. it seems silly now but at the time it was very important for kids in america to be reaching out for those things. she'd give away anything she owned, unattatched, knowing she could always buy newer and better with her parents money. none of these ideas had hit me prior to college, they were unknown where I grew up, where kids were removed from the cities and buried in little suburban haze—worlds, alive in spirit yet conceptually vacant.

yeah I remember Lordes, there's so much to tell about her, so much I've never even attempted to tell anyone. thoughts and memories that have rolled occasionally thru my head for years and years now. thoughts that have continued to seemed important. no-one knows these thoughts, nor could they know these experiences, which can merely be told. yet i grew up on stories, have learned from books all my life . . . false knowledge, maybe? all of it?

later, long after that impossible attraction i had to her, we were merely friends. i'd gone through a horrible lost and frightening hallucinogenic depression, fixated on the loneliness of never being able to have her. that night seemed like the end of the world. everything had me scared to death and at a complete loss, existence so far away. . . .

later, after we were just friends, and my intense wanting had passed, how easy it was then that we found ourselves at the end of a long day in her room, together on the bed, side two of 'dark side of the moon' playing over and over on the stereo, that woman's voice cooing a drawn out wail which had never struck me as being quite that sexual before. she didnt want a 'thing' made of undressing just wanted it over with. her beautiful nipples on a flat little girl body, shot still full of innocence somehow. her flesh so pure. that whole night such a single moment. i enter the memory museum. . . .

october eight
leaving denver

[VIC]   ah this is so soothing, this road stretching out in front, matte black and newly painted, little starry markers bordering both edges. tonight i look off into the darkness and wonder why the night and the road have such an appeal. on this night the sky is just a hollow shell, 'like tinfoil' said ken and that's about it, unreflecting. not giving anything back.

out in the ink tonight i see a pair of eyes looking back at me, waiting for me in the distance, down the road some ways ahead. is this the way of people passing? tonight i spoke to so many people, crossed so many lives, and yet i leave not carrying much feeling from it. it's as though walking through a fog that only clears at the end of the night, when all the people are gone. we give each other gifts of language. i am numbed by the amount of people with whom i can be caught exchanging a mere hundred words or so. how many can i go that small distance with, with no hopes of going further? what is this? books can't be trusted, and now even simple conversations are to be denied. what are we left with? crawling into bed as a way out, as a temporary relief. maybe that's better than nothing.

why is it impossible to say anything about love without feeling foolish? is it that it's such a tenuous and fleeting concept that we're scared to mention it for fear it will slip right thru our fingers? i have a devotion to a notion that keeps me from feeling the cold. i need to be with my son now, to have his small hands teach me about love, and faith and friendship. who'd've thought a little kid could do it? but now i'm parched and need a drink of life's youngblood. is that the allure of children? we get a booster shot, a fountain of youth.

last week in the attic of that house i saw a tiny white coffin with a face hole cut out for viewing the little dead child. what was it doing in that attic? was it laying in wait for some poor little kid, to torment his pitiful parents with? youth taken from the elders. . . . if this is the way my life is going to be, all this traveling, all these stages and places and people passing through, then i want him to see it while he can. what i wouldn't have given for this taste of life when i was a kid, instead of the iron-clad lock-up of an ordered suburban hell.

i travel this land and a continent across the sea, see these same hiways over and over again. no matter how softly they whisper they still tell me something of what it is to be free, even when they're trapping us with their denial of what true freedom really is. it's not the road that makes you free. there's no such thing as that kind of freedom, but it shows life, in its variety, shows that the scope of the world is what you take it for. pizante used to try to get us to see, most importantly, that reality wasn't a fixed view, but shifted with cubist facets depending on how you looked at it. we generally see things from one viewpoint only and that's the rut we get stuck in.

this is why we respect those with mental abberations, in some way they can flop between these varied viewpts, but it drives them 'mad'. they see too much. almost like seeing various depths simultaneously; you know, the molecular level mixing with daily reality. your hands would pass right through things. who could take a step? i want cody out on this road, to feel this reality, to glimpse this whole wide subtext at his early age. i lived in suburban shelter til the time i was eighteen, a hellish vacuum. no communication with parents, no conception of their world, sadly, we merely coexisted. no awareness of the thoughts in each others' lives, my mind held up in its shell. as soon as i knew how to think, their teachings told me somehow to turn it off and shut it up inside. what a sad state. is it the endless game of age against youth, or can i hope to have more communication with my son than i had with my father? how could he ever have hit me? blame it on the unthinkable rage of living in a hell himself, lost from all perspective on his life. nowhere with nowhere to go. what impotence to be able to chart the exact course of the rest of your life by the time yr thirty. how debilitating. he sunk into a world of sensations, hoping to blot out the truth, keep it at a good arms length. to this day he lives so far from the truth that he can never climb out.

can i feel certain in this reading of things? could it be that his little life, insulated from the truth, saves him the pain of concern or ambition, saves him having to lean or step on anyone to get somewhere? an equally sad fate, isn't it true, is the person who uses people as a means to more money? towards social position...

[PHIL]   life is fucked...

22 sept 87
texas

---

the reason a song heard on the radio can strike one so much more forcefully than the same song heard off a record or tape is that with the radio one has the over-whelming sense of intimacy w thousands of faceless others. ALL PLUGGED IN. a gestalt over airwaves, you can feel others grooving with you in a secret union. see-ing a movie in a full theatre as opposed to sitting in front of yr VCR at home. the crowd of plenty ties the mind.

"a big sky, as large as the mind, as loud and beautiful as heaven."

I THOUGHT OF YOU, SADLY
for M.G.

i'm not in love with love. new york city tonite and the whole thing is brought so much closer to home. the whole picture in a less-fuzzy frame. cruising 4 a.m. streets not knowing if i recognize this place or what. all the people in the club, they're new york but not the new york i knew, i guess that's gone already. which is real? this city with all this action and faces and words-thoughts-feelings? or this quiet fence around my head, drawing tighter each year?

kissing mary in the club, all that skin. . . . keep away mary, there is no need—to—burn here.

all this city, all these thoughts to grab hold of. why does crusing the NJ turnpike before dawn, all the lights glistening, seem somehow more real than friends and faces in front of me? does it hold more of that great emptiness that really is the world to see an empty highway?

all the mail, all the letters lost, and a voice says "i thought of you, sadly." what an epic thought there. all the straight talk in the world can't quench my thirst, or pull at this deep tone. the abyss, the crack in the world. i begin to slip through tonite. is this the dream? this ringing sensation behind my eyes? is it a passing myth?

"athens, her columns white like bones against the blue. . . ."

what is the thought that slipped away? all these stupid bldgs trying for a din to quench all thought. that blonde girl laughing and trying to come on. no hope in sight.

"i thought of you, sadly." you were part of my landscape. once i walked across yr back but now your memory in my head holds up a good part of the world, skies that have passed over me, ticking off years.

i slipped across yr belly
and landed on yr mouth
the instant thrill of you
some kind of NOW moves between us
like a river nearing its end
there's a time held somewhere just for us
if things go on long enough
so hard and hot/so sweet and wet

this theoretical affair we have
ramming you home in thin air
all the lonely eyes are watching. a world behind eyelids is turning on and off. in a
crowded bar all the images swirl and mix and when it empties out so does all the
hope. all the hopes stand staring at wishing their kiss on our lips.

eyes melt, glazed, unpolished, futile.
you love me a minute,
we can almost see clear to the end,
my face in yr hair, mine alone then.

legs
lips
neck
hair
all that skin

you got a hard on
i dont need one
you say yr no fun
i got a shotgun

everybody's building themselves an ocean
everybody's got their own little boat
they plan on leaving later this winter
heading away from the coast.

20 nov 87

Picture This:

Picture the poet standing alone in the rain; his suit wilted, bow tie ragged. the sidewalk wet, canvas awning rustling angry gusts overhead. In his thoughts, inside the tiny droplets falling from it, he's off in some blue world of quiet glades and rushes of wheat; prism fractured colors instead of gray concrete. While his suit gets soaked.

A man misunderstood, mistreated. Raped by the society that bred him in order that its integrity might be preserved. A standin for all men who have been suppressed. All who knew too much, who asked for the truth, who questioned too deeply. "Fucking crazy" they claim to protect their degrees. Who'd believe some old woman, or a foreigner?

Picture yourself in the ring.
Picture yourself the hero.
Picture yourself in two places at once.
Now you're NOWHERE at all.

25 mar 88

A Glimpse

me
ME
take me
see me
coming
towards you
let me offer
to you

a
glimpse
of some
embarrassing
moment
from my life
as proof of
my humanity
as though by
speaking of
masturbating
into a sock
or cutting
someone
wide open
with a dull blade
i could touch
some universal
chord.
some insect bite
on the soul
which you, too
might feel.

26 march 88
florida

Death, and Shellfish

when did i start eating clams?
when did my palate change?
i remember clambakes as a kid

my father and the other men
coming into the backyard
bushels of still wet clams,
from the bay
clam rakes against the shingles
the sound of knifeblade against
shell, sucking, cutting
i'd never touch one then
something i could never imagine eating.
when did all that change?
some time when i wasn't
paying attention
i acquired a new taste
did cigarettes have something
to do w this?
sometime when i wasn't looking
sitting around blowing joints
w michael and gerard and tim
in that rich kid's empty house
he was talking about music
i'd never heard before
i wondered how i'd missed it
what had i been doing?
now the only thing i seem to do
is worry about money, about death
about how to make things
with my own hands
how to make something of my life
amanda would like a house
she wants to leave the city.
it's not even my own death
anymore, either
there's cody to think of, first
i've made it this far, 32—
he's got so much still to go—
have to keep him safe

make sure he doesn't fall
off a chair
backwards
or drown in this beautiful sea
like my ma's brother charley
drowned at twelve
on a dare, off a dock
in brooklyn.
amanda is speaking pearls of wisdom
she says, as i write,
and i'm ignoring her
just to write *this*, she says
ignoring her, imagine!, to write THIS.
now the folks have come home
the wind is blowing
through the palms
outside the screen porch where i sit
the palms whose fronds
are turning yellow and
falling onto the sand
the palms whose coconuts are inedible
due to chemicals they've been
injected with
to try and save the foliage.
it's a constant worry
keeping cody safe
often i forget to keep my guard up
then i catch myself and wonder
how i'd feel if one time something
awful should happen
due to my nose buried in a book
or following those girls down the beach.
those young girls in their filmy suits
tubes of makeup, perms, raybans
sex wax tees
who are they dying to be?

once i understood, but it's
laughable now
a sorry state to want to be
twenty six at sixteen
when sixteen is so beautiful
just as it is
the maturity of age
can't be painted on, or donned
like a mysterious dark cloak of allure
these girls are looking forward
and missing NOW.
death, and shellfish
so much has changed.

**26 march 88
florida**

Keepers

If I could begin again:
they were all good years
all fine times
with good friends
and women, cars.
So I didn't achieve
an early sophistication
So I remain innocent
somewhat
to this day
Those times
were pure,
real as could be.

Times of insane joy,
with everyone together
when nothing moved
times of *being*

Yes there would be times
to throw out
but I doubt I'd want to
throw away all those days
cavorting around in the Volkswagen
in the woods
with Sue and Michael
the radio up loud,
the doors open, blasting
Dancing in the Moonlight
by King Harvest
high and in the sun,
or, for example, walking
a winter's night with
Thom, Jeff and Rob,
one night of many
shooting the shit
kicking an empty
vodka bottle which
we'd found—not drunk—
down Berry Hill Road.
Getting mad at Thom
for smashing it
against a dark wall
downtown
just for kicks.

Or right now,
doing nothing
listening to winds blowing
through the trees

hardly thinking at all
watching old movies in my head
so true to my depth

I've come this far already
there's not much money
but things aren't so bad
when I think about it.
and the light in this room
is soft and warming tonight.

26 march 1988
ft. myers beach

TIME PRESSES ME

1956 TIME BEGINS
1957 THE WORLD OPENS
1958 THE DAY GROWS
1959 HISTORY REPEATS ITSELF
1960 DAWN OF TIME
1961 REPLENISHMENT
1962 THE VOID
1963 MEMORY
1964 EMPTY ORBIT
1965
1966 THE PARADE ROUTE
1967 CANDLES
1968
1969 BESTOW THE SACRAMENTS
1970
1971

1972 THE WORLD SHIFT
1973
1974 THE TIDE IS HIGH
1975
1976 WE REACH THE TREES
1977
1978 CORNBALL REALISM
1979
1980 NEW DECISION
1981
1982 THE ABYSS
1983
1984
1985 TIME PRESSES ME
1986
1987
1988 THE MULTITUDE

29 march 88
ft myers bch

ECHOES

all of this life strewn before me:
sunvisors
books with poems
sneakers on weathered
floorboards
beach towels
magazines, piled high
on tables
today's paper

yesterday's paper
sand dollars
orchids
lawn chairs
buckets, shovels
wrappers
pillows, cushions
shells and sand
waves rolling
night sounding
echoes on the street

all this lies before me,
strewn about:
eyeglasses
chains
the telephone
boxes full of clothes
sandals and
long pants
the quiet teevee
Cody's red shoes
his books
fruitbowls
a clear surface
of dining table
all of it, haphazard,
very real and very
temporary, tonight:
tomorrow we pick up
tomorrow we leave here.

2 april 1988
holy saturday

MARK

He's still there. In the eight years since I met him he's never left the city. If it hadn't been for that photograph last night he'd never have entered my mind. I wonder what it's like, being a Brit and living in Berlin for so long. Within the walls. He's there now I'm sure. I'll see him again next year on my trip through. I can never recall his name, I have to work for a moment to find it. Mark. But I'd never mistake that face, that rail-thin build.

Can't be too pleasant, living so far from home for so long. I guess some people aren't bothered by those things. Happy anywhere.

What does he do with himself? He's wasting away there. So bright, so young when we met, with the luck of a transported national. Free of will. In that walled city where oppression hangs behind the facades. Such a wonderful thing to add a bit of tension to every single day, every little thing. We could use a little more of that over here. Things here are so boring, so sane.

The last time I saw him he looked older, I hadn't realized how much time had passed. He shook my hand through those heavy canvas work gloves. Smiled as though he knew me well. Made small talk as though I'd see him just days before. Standing there outside the cafe on Ku-dam. Of course I've aged too, no doubt about that, but somehow—he hadn't even left the city in all this time. I've been places. Made a few things happen to myself. Some things that might last. He's still hanging around, henching for Monica and Heiner. Getting thinner year by year.

I wonder where he goes at night. I've never seen him with anyone, I wonder does he have a lover? He must, I mean, Christ! That at least. That stupid fucking city. That jackass at the train station. How dare he cuff me. I had my passport. I was clean.

We said we'd meet the following afternoon, the day following the concert. At the restaurant near the movie theater. Querrelle was playing then, I remember that. But he never showed up. I waited thru two glasses of beer, it was a beautiful spring, then, so I didn't mind. He never showed. I had to leave the following day, I've not seen him since. Next year though, he'll be there. I'm sure of it. His pinched features, that British face, so fine and delicate. Milky white. I'm sure he'll be there then. I must arrange to spend some time with him the next time. get to know him a bit more. It's been a long time. I mean, who knows how we'll end up?

8 june 1988

a soldier, an epitath, a human spy

i can't find you
in this patch of sky
a soldier, an epitath, an island in heat
the matrix of yr delight, remember?

caught in yr lower depths
we freeze imbeciles, we read these clouds
you at the window,
me at the door
forever in debt
checking the stove
who wants in?

a dragstrip, a striptease
eyes meant to please you
a spider inside you
two steps away
your present is a mess,
a collar, a chokechain
a hung down ceiling

you waited all day
and couldn't say the word

we're here when you change your stain
we chameleon yr brittle fever-head
on Saint Marks the war is never over
i saw you there
shopping in the record store
getting louder as i watched
bigger, so far away
i can't find you anymore

DayDream Nation: Lyric Writing
May–July 1998

HEY JONI

Hey Joni put it all behind you
Hey Joni now I've put it all behind me too
These times can't add up, yr life is such a mess
Forget the past, and just say yes

Tell me Joni, am I the one, to see you through?
In this broken town can you still jack in, and know what to do?
I remember our youth, our high ideals
I remember you were so uptight
That time in the trees, we broke that vice
We took some steps and now we can't think twice

Tell me Joni, am I right by you?
Tell me how yr gonna lose this hard luck
Hey Joni, when will all these dreams come true?
You'd better find a way to climb down off that truck

Shots ring out from the center of an empty field
Joni's in the tall grass
She's a beautiful mental jukebox, a sailboat explosion
A snap of electric whipcrack
She's not thinking about the future, not spinning her wheels
She doesn't think at all about the past
She thinking long and hard about that high wild sound
And wondering will it last

There's something turning, Joni, turning right to you
My head burns, but I know you'll speak the truth

Hey Joni, put it all behind you
Hey Joni, now I've put it all behind me too

Forget the future, these times are such a mess
Tune out the past, and just say yes

it's 1963
it's 1964
it's 1957
it's 1962
put it all behind you
now it's all behind you

June 88

ERIC'S TRIP

I can't see anything at all, all I see is me
That's clear enough, that's what's important, to see me
My eyes can focus, my brain is talking, looks pretty good to me
My head's on straight, my girlfriend's beautiful, looks pretty
good to me

Sometimes I speak, tonight there's nothing to say
Sometimes we freak, and laugh all day

Hold these pages up to the light
See the jackknife inside of the dream
A railroad runs through the record stores at night
Coming in for the deep freeze

Mary: a simple word, are you there in the cold country?
Yr eyes so full, yr head so tight, can't you hear me?
Remember our talk, that day on the phone?
I was the door, you were the station

With shattered glass and miles between us
We still flew away in the conversation

My cup is full, and I feel okay
The world is dull, but not today

She thinks she's a goddess
She says she talks to the spirits
I wonder if she can talk to herself
If she can bear to hear it

This is Eric's trip
We've all come to watch him slip
He's slipping all the way to Texas
Can you dig it?

the sky is blue
the sky is the deepest purest clear blue i've ever seen
there's nothing more to it
and points on the globe are just...
points on the globe

I see with a glass eye, the pavement view
A shadow forming across fields rushing thru me to you
We tore down the world and put up four walls,
I breathe in the myth
I'm over the city, fucking the future, I'm high and inside yr kiss

We can't see clear, but what we see is alright
We make up what we can't hear, and then we sing all night

Skattered pages and shattered lights
A jackknife inside of a dream
There's something moving over there on the right
Like nothing I've ever seen.

RAIN KING

Rain King in chains has nowhere to go
His jetstream daydream cockshure hardluck show
His lips a fountain, his daylight sparks

He's a shotgun schoolyard streetwise white hot kid
With a whipcreem phonecall breakdown Rain King fist
His mind calls out the countdown, his daydream sparks

I need three years to clear these thoughts
I'd like to say I knew one true thing
It feels like years and all I've done is fought
And not turned up anything

Let the black day glow and roll over the bed
I'm waiting here for some reality crease
There's one big dead end in my head
And not a minute of peace

Crossfire Rain King with his Cadillac kid
Marries every dictionary from his trainyard bliss
His lips a fountain, his daylight sparks

Scattershot image king fortunate wheel when?
Keeps a steel drum wedding ring pontiac doorknob tent
His mind a countdown, his daydream sparks

Hung up on the speed king nation, caught up on a nail
Hangin' tight with time, at least a little while
Yr sister is a beauty when she's naked, like my kid
Out here in this whirlpool world dreamin' of a pitchfork kiss

IMPOSSIBLE GODDESS

yea, verily, we touch the goddess of light
red hair gleaming like a mutant catastrophe
we kept her up all night

all the things that she wanted,
all the things that she hides
you find it hard to resist

in the swollen moments,
where memory resists
there's an stolen hour
w her impossible kiss

all yr headline news
is just a bad print job
inside the black cat ruin
you got caught on the doorknob

knocked out in the jungle
knocked over the table again
her mystery is yr magnet
you rub til the end

all yr impossible demands
now they nip at yr heels
but she knows the future stands
while nothing is revealed

JUST SKIN

you were so different
on the telephone
than the one i remember

you so deep
the abyss of love
and i fear
i'll fall in

mystery is: the selection
vacancy is: the absence

the beating of my heart
is anticipation
the striking of a hammer
is a definite touch

yr jigsaw image now
that's the whole of you
just surface
just skin
how exciting
yr skin is

i see it:
the image of abandon
a tunnel of love
yr eyes conspiring
the rhythm of the tracks
the sound of a bell
ROCKING these streets

GLEAMING

blue suspension
empty coffee cups
cars glinting chrome
the radio on

radio:
all plugged in
grooving w you
across the airwaves
in a secret union

LA, all lit up, the nighttime gleaming
freeways moving into the city
country estates with guard dogs
freezing in the heat

A NATION REVEALED

prove my head
a nation revealed
all the years come free
prove my head
is a fortunate wheel
and call it catastrophe

prove my head

is up under the hood
the nation revealed
prove my head
is up to something good
a fortunate wheel

the pounding is a hammer
the sound is my heart
the end i remember
finished coming apart

i feel my head rush
caught up in the headlights
i feel yr body push
and everything's alright

how'd you get so hard?
where'd you learn to die pretty?
roll roll roll through the yards
like thunder rolls through the streets of this city

10 august 1988

The record at last is finished. Spent the afternoon w Nick at the studio cutting together the revised final version of "Hey Joni." Now it's all done and out of our hands. I'm in the air, in the evening, soon to be in Chicago. All the pieces that made up the mosaic of the last few months of work are firmly in the past. Four months of blurred movement. Looking for a rhyme. A cause célèbre. Looking for the right word, with which to say SOMETHING. I'm on the trail now. What is a voice if not to talk? Hafta tella bout things. Any things. Every thing. I'm taking from the voices that I hear, from the past and present. Dylan, Patti, Flannery O'Connor,

Springsteen, Thurston. All voices flow into the river that runs through my head. All words become mine once they are understood. All thoughts, all ideas are mine where I find them.

Raymond Carver died this week. What a sad blow. I feel like I just came upon him, and now he's gone. I saw him, met and spoke with him briefly just months ago. Now I hold that meeting more tightly in my memory. He didn't look too good then—couldn't breathe too well, but I didn't think he was that close to the end. His words spoke to me in so many ways this last year. I'm glad I told him so.

Now the end. Now the beginning. Things wrapped up, a new phase to untangle and discover. Soon begin the tours, the time away from home, the shows, the crowds, the talk and all the travel. Soon begin new things.

15 August 1988

Dairy Queen

We're sittin in the Dairy Queen about an hour west of Chicago when three young guys come in. Real sorry lookin guys, look like they been run over some, bent outa shape the whole of their lives. Ripped and dirty old tee shirts, jeans w no belts, barely hangin onto their butts, raggedy cuffs hangin over their sneakers. Come in for corn dogs and cokes. Sit in a corner booth and just talk quiet like they's out-siders in their own town. Beady little eyes takin everything in, ready to catch hell and throw it back in yr face. I can picture them sittin out under the highway over-pass, their bikes stashed in the bushes, takin pot shots at the cars and trucks whizzing by. With nothin to lose. Livin in cow-fuck nowhere, USA w nothin behind to push them up and nothin ahead worth carin about. So one time things snap and a driver gets hit bad, there's a bad accident, bad scene, and that's how it starts. A car slams into the concrete base of an overpass and suddenly without a moments notice there's no looking back. What's done is done and there's only to go forward, ride on out and try to raise as much hell as possible along the way before gettin dragged on down. "At least for a little while, yeah, we had us some fun."

SECOND SIGHT
second sight
mine tonight
every thing that's past this threshold
is now clear
every mistake stands out
in hard light
every knot
each misshapen image
every dust ~~mote~~ mote
all the dirt
grains of every hour drop
several sins are more
several roads have been left
several reasons in time
can be seen clearly
in hindsight.

Second Sight
1988–89

5 October 1988
Barcelona, 4 AM

To Cody

Well Cody I don't know if there'll be any way to explain to you what kind of stuff it is yr dad does for his living. I'm sure that at the very least it's not like anything yr friends' dads do! Yr half-way across the globe, three and one half years old. Meanwhile, yr 32 yr old dad is gesticulating on stages across Europe, letting anarchy (and occasional brilliance—ahem!) run wild for unbelieving audiences. Tonight felt like 1983 and our first European tour, when yr mom was with us, all over again. Songs were not played well, mishaps abounded, but a general tone and ferocity emerged, a SERIOUS and DANGEROUS fun, which I know was not what the crowd expected from a travelling band. They expected polish and song, they got Confusion and maelstrom instead. And they were glad. This was not/is not a normal band. Each night is a roll of the dice. It feels good to be more wild and less professional for a change. It's a great change, yeah. But how can you know? Will you ever see me in this insane state? By the time yr old enough to come along and really experience Sonic Youth, and retain the memory, will it still be there for you to see? I wonder. This is what yr father does, son, something not describable in terms of skill, or profession. Let's just call it performers and performance. It's the only word which takes the variety into account. Let's call it Hell Breaking Loose. Let's call it Out To Pasture. We can't always call it music, but we can usually call it Sound. Let's call it Volume, let's call it Sex/Noise. Let's call it Empty and Full all at once.

I wish you were here tonight, in Spain w us instead of back in NYC. I wish you could see what yr dad is doing with his life. The marks he's making. A night like tonight is really what it's all about. A new experience, for everybody. Not just a buncha songs. When this all ends I don't know where I'll be. It's not a fear I'll address here, now. I just wish you could know what yr dad is doing. It's pretty cool, I think, to have a dad doing this. I wish that I did. I hope you'll think so.

18 October 1988

The runway at JFK

Another tour ended, left to fade out into the past. All the items of interest passed—
a mere catalogue shall have to suffice—it went as before—travelling—planes and
fear of crashing—I'm up now, en route from London to NYC, and one crashed just
yesterday—a mere catalog here—no prose descriptions—it's all mundane—been
seen and done before—the roads once seen as an endless escape route to
freedom, now seem to lead to eventual destruction—car death more possible than
plane death—the height / the cliff / the drop—the flooding of S. France, our van
sliding off the road into the muddy ditch—those little roads through narrow
French-walled streets, flushed w water running brown as the Mississippi—every-
thing one same color—the buildings the land the water running up to begin to
cover the cars, the sky, all one muddy raw brown of clay of French earth—Dje-Han
w his mighty foot holding the brake down for 45 minutes until heroic French
truckdrivers (probably the nicest of Frenchmen are truckdrivers) pull us free neath
slate sky—singing RAIN in Eindhoven w Kramer and his Bongwater crew—
Farewell Angelina, like the Dylan song and so uncannily like a young Sue W., when
she wasn't speaking Dutch—Dje-Han w us in the insane late Spanish of Barcelona
night restaurant being served insane snails and gruesome delicacies of the seas—
hundred dollar ham sandwiches! Finding the Carver book in London—*Elephant*—
the last—and reading it just now w amazement here on TWA flight 701—Robert
Grima Spanish promoter—riding on Nick (the Greek's) motorcycle through
Athens—getting yelled at for stepping across the Parthenon ropes for a snuck
Greek SY promo shot—crazy alcoholic Cris like a giant dyslexic J passed out in the
Greek club dressing room—beautiful Isabelle through Spain sitting in mystery like
Sophia Loren waiting to make her first film—such a celluloid face! Her legs
stretched out on the bed—Spain like some insane western lands of cowboys
which smelled wonderful—which we drove and drove and drove across and
barely set foot upon the Spanish earth—I can now understand Hemingway's
feelings for this great country—Nick, so Latin so Greek, and Nana, and the gypsy
boys singing for us! Spain—Jane in England working out so well—finally in the fold,
and Liz—the shows—the volume the guitar swinging insanity of "Dog" in
Eindhoven w Epic and Rowland along, insane shows in Spain and Greece and big

shows for the world in London—fucking the future, bleeding the past, waiting to see what's next. Stoke-Newington. The Spanish waiters, and now, finally, the runway at JFK.

OCTOBER 29

heading to binghamton of all places, through the fall colors. rocky outcroppings gleaming against the clear of blue sky. leaves falling like stray thoughts, angels coming down. i'm all plugged up, cocooned.

OCTOBER 30

travelling through ny state—leaves all gone, real cold, it's snowing right now! last night was syracuse, carver's town, of sorts. was a botch-job. tabitha came. now it's to ohio.

the ride today has been exquisite. jamming down these roads with this jewel-like light and even the overcast skies rich with dark blues massed and drifting over the horizon. little roads running off to the sides, not going anywhere special, no distinguished ride there, just some old houses, a barn in the throes of deterioration, seen through the bare trees. browns and ochres all around, yellows and real GOLD. then the sun breaks through and the barn interiors are lit with stripes of beautiful light. it's getting dark now, over the brown dried fields, the light just a thin strip of pearl beyond the slopes in the distance. this is nothing you see in the city, this landscape. give me a movie camera and one hour of film, i'll just point it out the window: an hour of majesty. add any soundtrack you wish.

our headlights are gleaming off the silver back doors of a semi ahead. we saw three very serious accidents today, that makes four in three days. are we being told something? a sign, maybe? a car driven right under the back of a semi the other night, red flares showed the top peeled clear back to the boot. cars in the center medians, ambulance men still trying to get to the people inside; a giant semi completely flipped on the roadside, no-one anywhere around. and here we are setting out for six weeks on the road.

the sky right now is beautiful, steve points out. the deep blue clouds are rimmed in a fiery red light, almost crayoned-in across the great expanse. susanne says "it's just like that guy on tv who paints the pictures in fifteen minutes." "yes," i say, "it's that beautiful." thurston is screaming "the clouds! look at the clouds!" he's got his eskimo parka on and to him it's just like a hipgnosis album gatefold. yes, it's that beautiful. in this light even led zep on the box sounds okay. pay toll. don't veer off the road. move on.

NOVEMBER 7

in wisconsin travelling to minneapolis. snowy drifts in the fields. by tomorrow we'll be in the dakota badlands, and really in the west.

i'm about thirty pages from the end of richard ford's *The Sportswriter*. it's a strange and sad book in many ways, imperfect but very good. i don't agree with all of it but i like it a lot, and find it very comforting to read, somehow. the perfect drifting observations of impermanence that you want to read on tour. makes me feel right at home curled in my seat in the van, like this travelling life is somehow understandable, as good as any life. there's death and dying in this book—a dead nine yr old son—families together and split, divorces, suicides, sex and the promise of sex. the whole of a view of the world. a world as good as any, i guess it lets you see some good in any life, in yr/my own. anyone's. it also makes me feel quite far away from my own family, deep in these distant hills, far from the city and my home. makes me miss them, and my friends all the more. there's something early in the book about the friends you make when you grow up vs. those you make when yr little, the ones that really mean Friend. it made sense. it makes sense, this book. i like it, don't want it to end and will seek out his others before this tour is over.

tonight is the last night of the first leg of the tour. we leave Die Kreuzen and the fabulous Laughing Hyenas behind. larissa is the best guitarist i've seen in quite some time, really great great great. if john sang a bit more understandably i'm sure they'd grow to be very popular. the songs are good, the lyrics are too. as it is it's an amazing scream-fest blow-out every night. i really like it. it's over the indie edge. that first night it seemed larissa was the female rowland howard, the last guitarist i'd seen who really mattered a lot to me. but she's much more than that, i've come to see.

we're in the farmlands, the dairy country now, rolling and beautiful.

NOVEMBER 8

Today is the day for the convergence of feelings heaped up all through the last week. The end of the first leg of the tour. This morning a final breakfast with the Hyenas, last night a visit with Mary after the gig, conversation and a deep goodbye embrace with her. Now out in the dark cold of N. Dakota, Montana, all the way to the distant west coast of Washington State we roll. Goodbye to the Hyenas this morning, Larissa on tiptoes for another embrace, these people floating in and out of our lives, we're touching each other and then parting, like a book. I feel we left something with those guys, a good feeling and encouragement. John kept saying "This has been the happiest week of our lives!" and really meaning it. Kind of embarrassing but also kind of uplifting to think that such a thing is still possible just from a little generosity, interest and hanging out. Certainly we took what we could from them, no one-way street here, they are the coolest band, right up there w Dinosaur. I wish we were doing the whole tour with them. It has that feeling like when the movie was over out in Hollywood, a little group flung first together and then forced apart: just when you'd all learned to really work together and ROCK IT. Handshakes, kisses, hugs and addresses, and it's over.

Now we roll on, and those sweet kisses of friendship are gone on the winds of these high plains. Did it happen? Is it over, a thing of the past? Or still going on somewhere for us each/all.

Finished *The Sportswriter* another ending today in the van, a book that grew to be as a friend to me these last days, so perfectly in sync that as we pulled into Detroit, so did the book. If I could ever write with that straightforward and beautiful narrative style I'd feel I'd really achieved something. but no, it's too hard to explain feelings, it's a hard world to get one's thoughts together in. people around me don't seem too worried about it. It's hard to be natural, it's hard to know how to think truly and to actually SEE. I look but cannot see, feel but cannot touch, move but cannot gain any ground.

The visions and dreams all melt together again: One instant i'm with Mary, next Henry's on stage screaming, the dark hotel room with light shining in cool glow through the drawn-curtain in neon night, kids slamming in the pit, the amps so loud i can barely see, crashes all along the hiways as we drive through, the night sky full of stars, my body full of her and her and her, shitty food to eat, endless magazines to read through, a brass trumpet flashbulb. Narrative confusion, seems like a good thing to me, it seems to fit with this life. "Confusion boats, mutiny from stern to bow...", red lipstick, squeezing tight, a call to far-away home, squeeze tight kiss, lifting larissa right off her feet, both of us drenched in sweat. The crowd in nutty tattered tears, screaming around us.

What is a true sentence? An impossibility, that's what. I'm not buying it because i can't buy it, i don't have a true sentence in me. I can see the past now, something today made me think of SC, of old loves, i can't even remember what now. Her brother dying on his bike, a rebellion failed, buried with his leathers on. Bet that showed his jerk-off father some thing or two, his actually up and dying, to be free of his stupid family problems.

What happened in between? There's still a hiway rolling out of time in front of me. Could i live without it now? I told mary i hadn't been thinking about anything this last year, can't turn much up and yet my head is full, crowded with thoughts about every little damn thing, and then some. The thoughts of four or five different lives going on up there. Narrative confusion. Dialogue breaking down. . . . Mary said she had no friends, that G.'s boyfriends hated her because she could use the word "pussy" in conversation. Who has friends?

The cops would catch us for dope and let us go, emptying out the plastic bags onto the pacific coast hiway, liberating us from the paraphernalia, scaring the hell out of us, and then letting us go. They really didn't want me, no not M–E me.

It takes a true friend to help you turn off the world for awhile. Turn off the world awhile, turn off the world awhile, let it stop just momentarily so i can not think this minute, not talk these words, not move from this embrace.

We just passed Grassy Butte, North Dakota. "Imagine growing up there!" Thurston marvels. Roll. Roll. Roll.

NOVEMBER 14

just into california and rolling south out of the great northwestern rain forests in the night. i slept through most of the northwest. waking now and then to the most incredible landscapes coming in through north dakota and montana, then falling back to sleep. else we were driving at night, going 85 down the montana flats, not even aware of the canyons we were driving through until the next day. seattle was really good, i steeped myself in ray carver's country, found some new books with things about him, a tape of him reading, and even met a couple folks who knew him, and described to me the way his final days went down. tess came into the bookstore feigning happiness so no-one would know how serious things really were. read some local obits which also added bits of information. what a great loss, him dying just now. reading an interview with him gives the same wonderful personable feeling as his stories, you just WANT to listen to the things he says.

the northwest is interesting. i keep reminding myself of all the time jeff lived here. even the old-timers are old hippies, hand knitted wool sweaters, tye-dyes, long hair, no makeup, simultaneously arcane on the one hand, really outmoded, and yet still putting forth all these values of faith and trust. walking around the outdoor market today in portland, a little hippie haven, everyone was smiling and willing to lend a hand. young kids had sonic youth shirts they got at the gig last night, with mohawks AND crystals, tye-dyes and leathers. funny.

NOVEMBER 23

things have moved fast this last week or so. we're all the way to texas already. in another few days we'll be out of the west completely and back in the cloistered east. Los Angeles was a whirlwind, all the people, all the things to do, seeing Jeff and hanging out with him. it all happened very quickly and everything seemed to get spaced out while we were there (being able to stretch out in kim's parents house and all). it feels all the west is done already, the whole coast is over, san fran, the great shows of santa clara and LA, the fiasco last night of albuquerque, with the riot squad coming out, (nothing better to do). the west came on quickly and left as fast. we head back to florida and then on into the cold rains of the east.

NOVEMBER 25

deep central texas, hot and bright, riding in the van, everything as usual. yawn, who sleeps, who reads, who talks nonsense to liven up the dull daylight which cuts in through the windshield. freight trains roll by alongside, another book is finished, another dream tangential to the dream we glide through has just been laid to rest. all the cassette music sounds old and tired, even the ones we haven't heard yet. rusted trucks and cars sit idle, long idle, in fields off to the right just now.

steve has put neil young's "landing on water" into the ford's tape player, and the song "hippie dream" has just ended. we're on our way to austin. thurston is curled in kim's arms on the seat behind me in the van, nursing another morning headache while she reads iceberg slim. susanne is all the way in the back, her red head sleeping. i'm riding out a coffee jag and the thoughts of some few dozen "new" short stories i've lately read. ann beattie, richard ford, flannery o'connor, soon to include kathren anne porter, who wrote "pale rider", and chekov and cheever. always bringing it all back to carver, somehow.

as good as any of these stories get, none can measure up to his for clarity of purpose. while ann beattie's stories are quirky and seem to talk about a thing by describing all the happenings tangential to what she's actually trying to get at—a decent enough tack—carver simply draws a circle directly around what he's trying to say. so rich and economical, so perfect, like hemingway.

all these stories are filling my head, i'm trying to devour them, and figure out how it's done. what do you say to make a story? do you make the stuff up, write only about personal experience? what if you have no personal experiences of note? what if yr parents aren't divorced, or dead, or killers, or drunks? what if you've never been a heroin addict, or ran away from home, or lived by yrself for any real length of time. our culture leaves the well-off vacant and existential, and the poor angry and full of experience. i come to believe that the less fortunate have better, or at least more interesting, stories to tell, and that they are somehow lucky to have had all their terrible hardship experiences. instead of living it up shopping at the limited express in the north dallas mall, like that blonde i was talking to last night.

"come sit here and talk to me," she'd said, and that seemed a fine invite. she'd been to new york for a week once, studying "fashion" with a group from her college. she smoked marlboro light 100's and said she was waiting for someone, but i don't think she was. i read richard ford's stories and think that he must have grown up on the outs in that great big west, so empty of everything, so different from the east. when the men out here are drunk and the women stepped on, somehow it's a different story than it is back home. it would be funny to find out he grew up in massachusetts or somewhere, went to yale or tufts. i don't think he did, though.

where do these stories come from? i'm trying to decide whether to spend $300 on four hard-to-find carver books, wondering why i want them so much. why i feel the need to have them, and if the money is really important, or really not. $300 on four little books? will the fact that two of them are signed matter? that they are in mint condition?

i've come to hate conclusive opinions, maybe because i have none right now. what i at first hated about *the sportswriter* i finally came to respect: that the central character has many thoughts, but no definite decisions. he was buffeted about by life, and content to ponder the reasons why his girlfriend slugged him, or how he ended up a divorced sportswriter; he was drifting along.

maybe some have definite opinions and ideas. maybe it's admirable, but right now i have none, i can see nothing in this world that approves of the definite opinion. conclusive ideas bring power though—the force of having a theory to support, to hold up. i don't want the ideas, or the power. maybe it's my own failing, now. i'd like to be able to have some more real conversations with people, and say what i really feel. but often times there's nothing that i'm thinking of, just going through with what i have to do. especially now, driving in the van, mid-tour, we're in the doldrums and i'm just waiting for something magnificent to happen. if something magnificent ever does.

the other night we had just entered amarillo, texas, where those eight or nine cadillacs are buried in a field off the side of I-66, just a hundred yards from the road. amanda and i had stopped there some years ago when we were just aimlessly driving around out here in the southwest. it was night, everyone was hungry, but the moon was full. we could've stopped for a few minutes and just stood out there in the field with those half-hidden caddys and the sounds of the trucks rolling on the highways, and the lights of the city under the pearly moonlight. just to do it, anything for a new moment along the dull road. but no, most everyone saw no promise in such an action, they were all (except steve, who wanted to go, but wouldn't insist) too ready to find big twelve-ounce steaks in front of them—that was more important than the moonlight on some old cars in a field, stacked like giant rusting dominos to some old cowboy's monied whim. the moment that would've been worth waiting for.

NOVEMBER 30

i can't read any further. i look out the window and there's a huge white speedboat seeming to glide next to us, and then another, so close, all blue trim and chrome. both of them pointed up like rocketships about to spring from the carrier truck. we're in florida. flat veldt-lands looking not quite so odd as they have in the past. this many cars would make any landscape feel suburban.

susanne's glasses are so dark i can't tell if she's asleep in the seat behind me or staring right at me as i lean over her. motley crue is blaring from the tape deck up front, it's such ignorable music. here today... i can't read through its din. the stories are going by and all the significance is lost to the stream of the road. it's impossible to hold thoughts for examination in this existence. the only quiet time to think is in dark hotel rooms, and then it's too late. i'm too tired then.

all the stories i'm reading lately concern relationships: these things are happening in lives that got serious long ago, while we were still leading the lives of grown-up kids— living in rented apartments with other things on our minds than careers and families—important things like books, and records. *thought-dreams.* things like who's showing in which galleries this month, and are they any good? not sewers and milkmen, affairs with bank tellers and people who're mostly defined by what kind of job they have. *"oh, he's an accountant." "her husband's an entertainment lawyer."*

all the details fail to add up right now. there are no stories left with a hero who doesn't get torn apart. the little minutiae that make up our lives, how important are these things, really? right now none of it matters, nothing matters at all. each story goes by and each night of this trip is another one that rises and falls away. golf courses, red toenails, trailer parks. billboards, old sneakers, chain link fences. each with a story. each reflecting some facet of this life. a poem each. nothing. nothing. nothing.

i wondered where i was conceived. somehow it strikes me that it could have been here in florida on one of the many trips my parents used to take, before we kids were born and they fell out of that lifestyle. should i ask my mom? it feels somehow to be a strange question to ask. we never talk about those things. conception. certainly i could tell cody if he wanted to know. that we hit it on the first try, and couldn't believe it ourselves. i remember amanda coming into the room with the little test kit in her hand and telling me. our both feeling that, well, we were in it for real then.

let's see, i was born in february so i must have been conceived in early may of '55. it could have been in florida.

DECEMBER 5

this last week has been the south, moving out of texas and into florida for five vacant days. the clubs were only so good, the audiences only okay, even the landscape was bored this time through. i was pretty bored most of these days. maybe one or two of the gigs were okay. maybe.

this week has been cocaine, on many sides. down in florida it seems to be everywhere. it came to us through local emissaries, came to me as the subject of weird poem-stories through the mail, too; and then more the next day via tom. the sonic tom, not my thom. he who was my thom.

all the memories of these last days roll into a gnarly ball of fuzz. we shopped in athens all day today, with robert palmer soaking it up for rolling stone. some kids took us around atlanta today, day after our near-debacle hosting the last night of the punk-rock-hell-club. what a scene. we went up into the wooded hills of suburban atlanta (i just flashed on greece, a month ago we were in athens.) big homes set back on their own little hillock of prime real estate. the orange sun setting over the fountains and the bare trees. a barely tolerable juxtaposition. this guy todd had about a million rare records in his parents' basement, about two thousand of which we managed to get him to "trade us" for sonic promo items we will send from back in new york. incredible stuff, sun ra, charlie parker singles lying next to rare per ubu, beefheart, neil, theremin records, you name it. it was a strange day sifting through all this fanatical vinyl debris.

i wandered upstairs from this huge concrete basement and ran into his father standing, just staring out the window at the trees behind his house, standing on the large-tile white tile floor that swept through the living room and into the kitchen. nice pictures on the wall. everything real neat. we talked and then i went into the bathroom. why are the bathrooms in big pristine houses such a mess? dirty rings around the tub, shower curtains all stained.

i realized that what i need to do in order for this writing to really mean anything is to try and get at those thoughts that i never choose to write down, the things i hide from everyday view. the things i keep inside only me. i know what these things are. all the catholic guilt. all old memories. thinking. listening. not aiming at anything. nothing i will tell here. i decided i'm not ready to write that good.

i saw ann beattie's picture today on some dust jackets in a gigantic bookstore and decided that even though i really liked her book, she looks like the kind of woman i would have absolutely hated, in college. so i'm having to reassess. nobody knows who the hell Carver is. bookstores all across the country since texas have not even known his name, practically. yet the books lauded him so highly. "a modern master", the dust covers tell the readers. no one knows him except the collectors. i guess i'm glad. a little privacy for one's hero.

we met harry crews in jacksonville, kim interviewed him. even the beach there in florida, (which i walked both at night with the b.a.l.l. dudes as they were wondering about the breakup of their band, and again in the bright sun of late morning before we left) was just okay, the water was rolling in kind of a mashy green color, and the waves sounded kind of fuzzy, and distant. bird shit all over the sand.

b.a.l.l. were breaking up and arguing like children for a couple of days, but i think the sleazy promoter jerk-off pricks at the metroplex kinda united everyone again in battle against the real evil scum: the promoters and club-fuckers that touring bands have to deal with. so they were laughing together at eve's end in atlanta. all the town was in joy. the streets sat easy. we took off. we slept. downslide halted. we set things upright again.

19 january 1989
melbourne

First australian gig tonight. We've been out on the streets today, walking around the shops. Not much going on. Not much narrative action. There's not really much out of the ordinary that happens in this life-style. From the outside maybe it looks quite adventurous, all the travel and opportunity, but from inside it's just one day after another. In one club after another, the same rote pattern. Meeting people after the shows, the cool ones, the interesting ones, the pretty ones, the weird and fucked-up ones. the faces change from night to night but the pattern of the thing remains fairly stable. It's not very interesting after awhile. Talking to interviewers, talking about books etc. is the most engaging part. I'm actually speaking my mind, dredging up thoughts for someone who is writing it down, whom is interested, at least partially, in passing those thoughts on. But sometimes I'll find myself talking to someone whom I know is not getting any of it, or just reciting answers by rote to questions I've answered dozens of times before. The playing is the one thing that doesn't go stale, and I guess that sums up the reason for continuing. The music remains enthralling, the act of playing, the end result. Mining the sonic depths and coming up with a plum.

Occasionally a relationship will arise, something which lasts more than a few hours. Amidst the detached life of working and staying ahead in the game comes some feeling of camaraderie, some communication. Some deep gazing. Some night unfolding.

Otherwise we're just another form of travelling tourists much of the time, exploring book stores and record stores mostly instead of museums and ruins, although sometimes those too. Once it seemed very exotic travelling to all these far out places, but really one gets little more than a brief flavor of each, and even that on the run. I opened Hemingway's posthumous book "The Dangerous Summer" in a store today. it begins with a line about how he never thought he'd return again to Spain, a country he loved more than any but his own. That one line indicated a relationship with a place, a deep feeling of having lived in a place and really felt its richness. That's a feeling that has not really come over me in all the travels we've done. Maybe Holland, where I've spent more time than elsewhere, but I don't get the feeling within me that Hemingway conveyed in his line. Maybe I'm just not capable of it. Maybe my life is so full of daily distractions that such a poetic feeling, such a rhythm within life, is not possible.

23 january 1989
melbourne

i met a young girl named robin last night, and her mother. a mother and daughter team, down in the beach community at ocean grove where we played. i'm not sure what they were all about, where her husband was, etc. probably a divorcee. they had that women-travelling-alone feel. mom kind of young, frosted hair, smoking cigs and joking with her daughter in an almost sisterly way. and robin, seventeen, a pale-skinned beauty with a shock of dark carefully cut hair, beautiful long neck and dark eyes, unblemished, about to explode into adulthood. about to leap. i ended up at their cabin talking to them awhile, about australia, the states, the group, just talking away into the darkening night, big dark clouds rolling in over the moonlight. hanging back-lit in the distance. it was pretty cool to talk to some new faces, outside of the daily group. i was under the spell of this young girl, she was so beautiful to me, although of course it was mostly the situation and her youthful age, how unblemished she was. still a child really. i became infatuated with her, one of those dreamy longings that almost always remains just that—a dream, something to ponder. at one point i wasn't sure which of them was the more interesting, the mother or the daughter, but robin's beautiful youth won out. the only problem was separating her from her mother there on the porch. finally mom hurried inside for awhile to tune in the australian open and witness pat shriver lose her chance to move up. in those minutes as we two talked outside the door, i recall watching myself stare into her eyes and look at her lovely face, as the yellow light of the room spilled out into the blue night around us. just a brief scene, a moving picture, nothing momentous, but a wonderful sight none-the-less. meeting her set my mind thinking about all manner of things too lengthy to expound upon here, at this hour of the night.

25 Jan 1989
adelaide

[conversation]

> i came from perth to see you
> from perth! really . . . that's pretty far, isn't it?
> yes, it sure is. i don't know a soul here in adelaide, pretty sleepy town this, eh?
> yeah i guess, it's alright, we went to the zoo today. . . . perth, that's like travelling LA to Chicago or something. . . .
> is it? i dunno, it could be. i've got a hotel room here and some good speed and a good book, you're the first soul i've talked to since i've been here.
> how'd you get here?
> well i started out to hitch and got about 700 k's, as far as [unintelligible], and then i stood in the heat and about a hundred cars passed me by, so i said "fuck this" and took the bus the rest of the way. i'm going to fly

back tomorrow, maybe.
is that thru the desert to get here?
well not actually the desert, more like scrub plains, not desert like the great
      sandy desert, i've never been there but i assume that's real sand desert;
      this road comes down from perth and then goes straight east to here,
      you know the great australian bight? the land goes down and then rises
      in this bight, well the highway goes straight across the top of it.
uh-huh.
can i hang out with you this evening? you're the first persons i've talked to
      since i've been here. . . .
well, i don't think we're going to be hanging out very long, we've got to drive
      towards sydney tomorrow, but until we leave, sure. . . .

there's good dope in sydney. . . .
what?
good dope in sydney. . . .
oh.

27 january 1989
wagga wagga

2748 BRIGHAM STREET, BKLYN:
the kitchen, the food, the family. all the young kids (me among) spinning in the
middle room, the bedroom. the musty parlor thick w overstuffed ancient chairs
and dust filtering in the sunlight. the family, the kids, the relatives all crowded in
and talking loudly, all at once, everyone speaking, no one listening. the people
who lived in the apartment off the hallway, whom i'd always thought were just
more family when i was very small. the great porch with green canvas awning in
the summer, the bocce court, pear trees, rotten scrub lots awaiting developers
where we'd catch lightning bugs in jars on summer nights, the glitzy Four Seasons
mobster restaurant, the wine, drinking, arguments, linoleum floors, always food

cooking on the stove.

SHIFT FOCUS TO LOCUST AVE OR IVY STREET:
the thanksgiving table, the piano, everyone still talking, little candies set out in dishes shaped like leaves, the chill blue days, Eric slamming the door, drinking and cooking in the kitchen, cursing, fighting with Maria, midmeal leaving abruptly to walk in the cold night air, leaving the gabbing women behind. my father sleeping in a chair. crisp pre-snow winter atmosphere. sometimes i'd go along for the walk. never sure back then just exactly what was going on, who was mad at whom, and who was right or wrong. but outside in the snowy or near snowy night air, everything seemed much better. it seemed the right place to be.

1 february 1989
sydney

i'm filtering out. . . . falling out, can't think straight. i can see various viewpoints, wasn't that the idea? they leave no road left. the multitude of directions nullifies the significance of each single one. can that be? cowboy movies on televison. do we look like cowboys now? got the right boots on? does the look fit the day? or should it be a bit more . . . purple?

what would be the best thing that could happen?
i just don't know.
where is this all taking place?
not sure. are we in the head or in the world?
can't say.

voices speaking all over the place, out of every mouth and speaker. have you noticed there are few places without one or the other anymore? Not enough gaping silences. no peaceful schussh. this fine city is only a backdrop. why does hearing the cars going home over the hills at dusk here frighten me. their false permanence. their happy little lives. shy faces. we asked directions from the van window on the street today of a woman, mid thirties—hey is that our age now?—her voice had a particular sound, her movements and mannerisms so strange, her personal "normal." i couldn't get over it. her whole life, and i can't understand a word of it. i asked myself as i listened to her, who talks like this? whose world could have brought them to this point? i hadn't a clue. she was so normal that she was an alien to me. some girls are singing loudly on the street now, voices raised and bubbling. everything's exploding, nothing's moving. everything's arcing towards the light in incredible slo-mo.

sly boy goes off with the teacher, straight and to the point. shy boy misses the dancer, stumbling through too many steps. slo-mo boy loses the willow girl to the trees. i'm told you can't beat the feeling of her green ride. her high tide. her soft thigh.

i've been reading so much it's given me a headache. my file catalog is full, history is escaping as we speak, air from a puncture wound. put two and two together for me and let me see the result. are you sure you have an answer? didn't they show you there's no such thing? no ultimate purchase? no best punch line ever? fuck what the fuck shut up shut up torn off turn off turned off driven off driven out out out shut out put out hung out clothesline pole—hole. hole—in—one they're chanting. no political notions in mind. no life saving clock ticking in the background. what are we talking about here, anyway? nothing nothing hahaha nothing and we know it! (they're still singing on the street, chanting songs with the radio-wave formations flying around them.) does this time period belong inside or outside of parenthesis? tv on the proper channel? he's playing the cello. chellow. the last book i read started with three quotes, none of which belonged to the book's author, in order, i assume, to set the framework for what was to follow. the longest of these quotes was written in an ancient, now-dormant style. i couldn't get through it. didn't know what old will shakespeare was talkin' about. a figment of someone's head? a cotton crown?

if you could only see one television commercial again, ever, in your life, which one would it be? if you could choose a mate for life, like the whales do, could you or would you do this? if you could recall only one conversation, ever, again, could you jot it down and send it to me? send pictures if you can, especially if she was pretty.

robert palmer is talking to a virgin on the teevee right now, it seems he's "got to get up." was that virgin or version? funky guitar breaks. obscure as all hell? sure. up early? not certain. not cretin. not curtained. not certain, no no no, and i forgot to pick up the phone. sleep sleep sleep sleep sleep sleep sleep sleep sleep sleep sleep sleep sleep sleep sleep. sleep.

in her pink sweater she said "i woke up in the middle of the night, three in the morning, and found myself standing across the room looking at my things, not knowing for a minute where i was, and seemingly about to write out some checks, or something. . . . it was weird."

after that she was moving and doing little dance steps there on the street in time with the giant video screen inside the bar. her mouth in a little pout.

3 february 1989

queensland

it was a full day, yesterday. he thought back to his trek with S. and C. down the buttes from the lighthouse to the sea, to where it was storming up over the rock outcropping at the land's end. they were out amongst the rocks, which were strange and sharp-edged, as though a forest of vines and dead leaves had heaped high and rotting before being compressed into stone. the ghostly shapes of ancient plant forms were still visible in the rock. a huge wave roared up from behind and drenched the three of them, and then, some minutes later, when they had forgotten the beauty of the raw sea coming and going, its voice a deep thronging sound captivating them, it happened once more, and they were then thoroughly soaked. the climb back up to the lighthouse was more direct—up the near-vertical grassy slope, rather than the long and traversing steppes they had descended. he had to stop and rest near the top, heart beating wildly in his chest. but it felt good. especially upon turning around and seeing the promontory where they had just been, white water roaring, always and forever roaring away at the rocks. he could see the breakers far offshore commencing their white rolling surf, then ducking under the surface until they would reemerge closer to the shore to finally, fully rear up before the cliffs. farther off, out in the deep water there was a small volcanic island, all rock and no green, and as he watched the sea seemed to move in reverse as well, to the horizon in a massive undertow to crash up against it as well. through this same cold sea he had seen the great humpback whale migration not four months ago. soon they would be returning through here once more, but he would not be here to see when they came.

later that day he was driving up into the hills, in the car with M. and T., until they were riding along a green crest with the world stretching out with miles and miles of pasture and rainforest on either side of them. up and still higher they drove, through the banana plantations and cow fields before finally turning back at the crest. one kilometer further along, down a well-kept though unsealed earth road-way, they arrived at the farm. horses grazed about the grounds, unpenned. beautiful young steeds. all was quiet here, back from the highway. he thought how many stars there must be at night here. that was the first thing which struck him. through a complex of various small buildings they drove on, stopping at the last in line, where some few other cars were parked under the leafy trees. they found the couple they had come to see in a small wooden office tacked onto the back of the main building. as they came around the corner, still marveling at the endless rolling landscape, he watched as a trail of cigarette smoke slowly uncurled out the window. Vladimir came out to meet them, an aging hippy with long grey hair, blue jeans and boots, fringe jacket and a black felt hat from the outback, adorned with hammered silver birds. Lil appeared a moment later at the window, talking through its open pane as they sat on the rail fence there behind the office. she had jet black hair and lots of kohl around the eyes, still quite lithe, quite good-looking. thin, fine legs covered with skin-tight leggings. full breasts under a loose black shirt. a dancer's body, she later informed him.

they all smoked and talked like that for awhile, she inside and the rest of them out-side, and then the men all moved into the office where Vladimir spilled large lines of coke out of a vial and onto the glass desktop, pushing aside the heaps of books and paperwork, the reels of recording tape. when he talked it was in such a hushed whispering wheeze that they had to fight to stay on top of what he was saying. but mostly Lil talked, her conversation whirling off in one direction and then the next, ignoring Vladimir's interjections, pausing the main flow often to parenthesize, or make a brief aside on some tangential subject. talking an endless stream, staring straight at him all the while, shifting her legs back and forth under the desk. he marveled at her ability to always thread her way back to her original topic, long after he'd drifted off into simply watching her flashing eyes, lost in her stream. she kept talking about the hippy community who mostly inhabited the surrounding area, talking about "them." quite sure she was not one. yet her speech was peppered with cosmic slang, "sitch" for situation, used over and over, as in "you know their sitch, right?" between her hybrid accent and the fluid nature of her conversation, one word rolling into the next like a heavy drinker, it was hard to stay with her. Vladimir was passing around a joint now, and her 14-year-old-son Luke had brought in a bottle of good champagne from the fridge, and fine cut glasses were filled and went around as they talked. Lil ordered her son around as though he was her manservant, although they were good natured about it and seemed very close. She told us about Luke's band, in which he was the drummer, and they chatted for awhile longer before it was time for the three of them to get back down into town. They left saying they'd see each other that night after the show.

that night the show went well, easy and low pressure. there was hardly anyone there really, about two hundred people in a one thousand seat hall. but it didn't matter. the mood was good, relaxed, and those who were there were in on the joke of the poor attendance, the absurdity of coming all the way from the states to wind up out here, in this beach resort in the middle of nowhere. they played for fun, almost in relief from the packed houses of late, and the crowd enjoyed it. a good night.

afterwards the backstage rooms began to come alive. various people coming in to talk, asking for autographs, interviews, advice, opinions. when things really got going M. and he snuck off to finish the last of the coke they'd brought back down with them from the farm. it was, for once, an additive high, getting better with each line. usually he found that after the first rush of the drug was through, no subsequent amount could regenerate that wonderful chill feeling. but tonight was different. with each line a delicious feeling of freedom rolled through him. when they returned from the bathroom, Vladimir and Lil were there in the dressing room along with the other well-wishers, his mind began to turn with the thought of just a bit more, a bit more which he knew Vladimir must have on hand. he spent a long time that evening listening to the two of them, Vladimir mumbling and Lil babbling at him.

"how was the toot?" Vladimir wheezed, under his breath.
"oh, pretty good, yes, but it's already all gone." he replied, hinting obviously.

it wasn't really unpleasant, listening to them, although he found himself drifting off in his head, and thinking about the coke. whenever someone else in the room would come over to talk or drag him away for a few minutes he welcomed the relief. but everyone was fairly boring anyway, that night, nothing seemed that interesting or urgent. he found himself drifting again back to Lil's flow.

now she was talking about astrology and sun signs, going on and on, talking about how she and Vladimir were a totally different pair than she and her (ex)husband had been. Vladimir was a Leo, her other husband was a Sag.

"i'm Aries, so you know that sitch, right? i'm not one of those nebulous people, nebulous, that's my fave word this week, nebulous, because it means nothing, i'm not one of those who would or could walk up to someone and say, oh yeah, i know, you're such and such, right? like one night i had this woman—they always seem to be women, right, in this sitch—she came up to me and said, oh i know you're a cancer, and she proceeded to tell all about myself as a cancer, and so of course i went along, right, didn't wan't to blow her scene, it wasn't worth it, right? that was her sitch, so i couldn't guess your sign, tell me, what is it? i couldn't guess it or really have a clue about it unless i knew you for a very long time, then maybe it would be cool, obvious, right? what's you're sign?" she paused, finally coming up for air.

"Aquarius," i said, "i'm Aquarius."
"ah," she said, "water."
"actually i think it's an air sign," i said.
"no, no, water she said, i know it."

he let her have her way about it, not being absolutely sure himself.

things went on and on. he drifted in and out of various conversations, moving around the room, having another drink and thinking about the coke. he knew if he waited long enough it would happen. finally M. suggested with a great deal of finesse that everyone head downstairs to the bar for a round of kiwi daquiris. it was very late by this time, he was ready to crawl off to sleep soon, which he knew he'd never be able to do on any more coke. M. ushered the crowd off until only they four and T. were left.

"allriight, M., good show," sighed Lil, "i thought we'd never be able. . . . " Vladimir immediately brought out his vial and began slashing large white lines onto the tabletop with a card. he rolled a bill and took his first, handing the bill over to Lil next. she was in mid-sentence and kept talking for a few minutes before finally bending over to whiff up a few lines. he hadn't heard a word she'd said, although she'd been staring right at him. he was watching her hand holding the rolled up bill, and waiting for her to pass it to him. which she now did, although not before she'd finished her thought. he bent down and snuffed up a few lines of the stuff, handed over the bill to T., and sat back down to let the feeling rush over him. for some moments he drifted off. when he opened his eyes M. was herding the rest of them towards the bar. he stood up, finally, alone in the room, and started for the door. in the hallway he found Lil emerging from the bathroom, eyes flashing now from the coke.

"is everyone gone down?" she asked, motioning him inside.
"i have some more. . . . "

he followed her into the bathroom where she quickly cut out four more lines. she did two and then handed the bill to him. he bent over the counter to take his share. her hands came around his waist as he finished. she pulled him up, turned him around to face her. her eyes danced, and she rocked her head back and forth in a little dance. next he knew she was kissing him, her tongue rolling around his mouth, her lips soft, rubbing her body up tight to him. she ran a hand across his crotch, and began giggling, grinning at him.

"good coke, isn't it?" she smiled. "Vladimir always gets the best."

they found the others at the dark wooden bar, already drinking. Dimitri and M. had slipped off and came into the room moments later, M. grinning ear to ear. he was bored of this, and although he knew he couldn't sleep he slipped away as soon as he had drifted to the edge of the crowd, going out the steps and into the darkness. she was babbling to someone else, one ear as good as the next, as long as someone was listening. they'd probably be there drinking for quite some time.

he made his way back to his room, but sat outside on the bench beside the door. the air was cool and still, the moon down. he could faintly hear C. and S. sleeping inside the cabin. he knew he wouldn't be sleeping for quite awhile. he could feel his heart racing. nothing mattered. he didn't want to talk to any of them back there. he didn't want to write, or to think about anything. none of it mattered. his mind was racing from topic to topic, unable to hold any thought. fantastic flashes racing through his head, stopping only long enough to peer out from the shadows, but not long enough for him to get a hold of, to contemplate. he couldn't hold anything just then. where was he? even that became unclear. halfway around the world, under the southern cross. that much he could see. he could look up and see the stars, the cross pattern high above him in the east. the tiny points of light were still, and his head fell back and his eyes drew them in. these he could hold. here was a place he could linger awhile. this felt good.

13 february 1989
kyoto

kyoto night
trains runnin at bullet speed
temples glowing with love
silky japanese girl
face an ornamental gem
the golden pavillion
slow silent fascades

simple ruins and saturated rhymes
these japanese girls
so fine featured
unblemished
faces without sadness
submitting
forgotten
without fear
kyoto of temples golden
and buddhist monks silent
green mossy gardens
stoned theaters
ancient woods
bamboo forests
mossy greens
the softest carpets
the water harp
light streaming
words tumbling
visions arriving
dressed in black
to seek perfection
the silent running of the leaves
flush with the wind

30 April 1989
New York City

A Bit of Memory

summer's almost on
the diamond days ahead

i can feel it
the need to immerse
to pull under its cover
its foggy haze

i can take it all in
and open the gate
throw sand in the cracks
and watch it filter down

this is the end of the day
these are the times of our lives
talking, hoping
laying in wait
trying to stumble across something sensible.

all the boys tighten their belts and
stick it to each other.
who is on top?
and who is in place?

open the papers
and tell me the news
light up the pages
WAIT for tomorrow
climb down off that truck

Ignition:
charged up
screaming in the din
waiting for nothing
I REMEMBER EVERY WORD YOU SAID
each time we meet
I can't remember
yesterday
but I can remember

ten years ago
when nothing was important
and everything mattered
QUITE A CLEAR PICTURE
the back porch was so significant then
gleaming glasses on sunlit tables
green and gold and brown
you said nothing was important
and everything mattered
epic discussions
and then
I'd meet you in the bedroom
sliding across your body
late in the night
while they're talking next door
through thin walls
under low lights
meeting in the bedroom
and not speaking a word

a dead end world
of memory floods
ideas under water
wet as stones
all the machinery rusted
till nothing was left
our house itself raised
I set up a room on yr porch
it was summer by then
the cats slept in the middle of the driveway
the light shot straight through the pines
from Syracuse all the way to Binghamton

a room for me on yr porch
you danced around me in that room
the last time I really had friends

was the last time I really had none
a group without enmity, ended
they tore the house down
and tarred it over

Memory is an epic poem, an endless story, the details shifting in place. Hazy light on dim faces, photos turning grey. I need a fulcrum to lift each day now, to elevate need to a burning desire. I remember the pressing need, the longing, the beautiful empty feeling of wanting, of being incomplete. But that was long ago. I can't remember how it went. Now nothing matters, and everything, every damned thing, is important. Memories are forever backing up, mixing up, jumbled and unclear. All that i have left to strive for, each event these days, means less and less. And yet every damn thing is so important.

17 May 1989

Almost nothing quite as nice as sitting on a moving train, watching the world roll by, listening to other people's conversations, destinations; no better time to get some thinking done. Except these days I can't think of anything at all. My mind is blanked out. Overloaded. I can't make any connections at all right now. I'm watching a movie without a soundtrack. Or a plot. Kneeling in front of the coffin at the funeral home, I was barely cognizant of there being anyone inside, let alone someone I knew. All I could sense was the spray of flowers in my face, at my knelt-down-eye-level. I couldn't bring up any feelings, not even for a moment, a glimmer of sorrow. How does that song go? "Life . . . da dum da dee dah . . . Life is Life. . . ." Even that would've been a handy thought had I been able to think of it.

Luckily I didn't have to say much to anyone. I offered my condolences to Tom, Sr., and then Thom and I, both of us in our suit jackets, made for the lobby where we could talk. Just rambling conversation, my clearest image is of a little black insect crawling across the lace curtains in that hot foyer, the sun beating patterns across the sills. I would've liked to get my movie camera from the car—those curtains, I'd decided, with the light burning across them somehow summarized my feelings, and the mood. They will now be bound up with my final thoughts of T's mom. But no, no movie camera here amongst the elders, only Thom would've understood the impulse on such an occasion.

We rambled and talked generally about our place in the world, our old town streets outside, some faces from H.S., our families, our own little lives growing and passing. "Like waves," Thom said of the endless cycle. Yes, waves.

We talked for awhile about travelling, alone, the need for it, the desire to do it. I've hardly done it at all, feel very insulated. All my far flung travels always amidst some tour group, some mass of people grinding individual experiences to a halt. Putting it all in the mind.

Thom's done some, although not for quite awhile. We talked of the past, as always, although we're both well aware of our present these days, we don't dwell like once we did on things gone by. I told him I felt pretty sure of our group friendship now, was not worried about drifting out of it, either locationally or mentally. Amanda had remarked to me "you mean his dad and yrs grew up together just like you two guys?" and although they were not as close in age, yes, they did grow up together, on the same street no less. both of those houses are still in our respective families. It's a funny thought. Yaas, we're friends from way back, it's true, and not dictated by any sort of "working" or "business" relationship, either. We just talk, as always we have, about everything, the past, the NOW, to future near and far, all manner of things which often exist only when their talked about. Ideas which coalesce out of smokey words and hover just overhead only so long as the dialogue lasts.

So we talked awhile, in the sunny foyer and outside on the porch railings, with our old town coming and going about it's business around us. About the southwest, about France, and Germany, about how we've burned out bridges behind us, about how we'll never live in a small town quite like this one, where everyone that comes in knows his family, and mine, and "Oh, you must be Nick's son. . . ."; how all the lives here are entwined. "We grew up with yr daughter, Tina, Mrs. Sangermano," we said. "Oh yes, she still works in Buckinghams, just down on

South Street, still lives here. She's married now and has a family." So have we, but we've left, we're gone from here, into the great world outside.

4 july 1989
nyc

I can't, I just can't bring myself to sit and write now, there's too much happening, too many books to read, thoughts to think, calls to make. Everything is a great BALL of mixed-up emotions and crossed wires. I'm thirty-three! What the hell am I doing? I have so many questions, but no patience to sit down methodical and enumerate them. I'm a musician and yet sometimes I can't hear, the absurdity of the whole mess, having run headlong and headstrong up against the physical walls, blinded (deafened!) by the sheer exuberance of making sound. But now those sounds have all vanished from the planet, the waves created by all those gigs from the O.P. in Binghamton to the Mudd Club through to Australia and Leningrad have left the planet—expanding outwards into the universe. They're gone now and sometimes I come up feeling empty-handed. Nothing at present, my sense of accomplishment tarnished by the impending future. But I'm lucky, I know this, and too hard on myself. I can (and still believe it) succeed at anything I want to. So why fear the future anyhow? Where are we going? How will we live. Gotta make hay now, yet as always I'm caught in a maze of small things, little details that weigh down on what I want to get to.

My dad came home today, tears in his eyes at the threshold, my mother said; the doctors' have given him a new chance at life, a whole new existence, he should be dead yet he's saved for now, to go on with his old age. What feelings such events must draw forth! Yet I never consider him to have feelings he's been so careful to hide them for so long; he's a bull, internal.

My large script here reminds me of Linda S.'s handwriting. That rush of energy across a page, and of things, other things still to do that were once behind the words. Memories flood in. I can't reach Jeff in Seattle (unlisted). Thom is still here but sometimes adrift in a world so illogical I can't fathom it. New rehearsal sessions have started. Carver's final—WATERFALL—about to come out. I want to write about it. 'Nother solo rec? Big record companies and managers and the parting of ways with loyal friends now useful no longer, crossroads now coming forth.

This is what I think about it: Whatever happens next, success or failure, is just gravy. This is beyond the point where our plans and goals left off. Deep space. We have, w DAYDRM, accomplished all that we set out to do—the world knows and respects us, we've proved we're very good at what we do, maybe even better than that. We've ascended to the top of the "underground, independent" heap. All has been fulfilled. Now we're off the page. Garnering huge chunks of new experience in areas we'd never imagined (really) entering into. How can these majors seriously expect to sign 6-8 record deals w bands who have 6-8 yrs of history behind them already? They're really foolish, but I guess they only have to hit one in ten to profit. (And that's what it's all about.) The 'gold watch' they offer in the way of *past achievements award* is lovely, but they should be realistic.

The underground knows what we do, most of its insiders are bored with what we do—they've been hip to it, so we've a new larger more uneducated audience to attend to: Who knows what will happen, but it'll be different than playing for your friends. I don't care what happens next, if we rise up, play lounge jazz, who likes us, what category we fit in, who thinks we're over, whatever. We (for my part) will play for ourselves now, I'll play whatever style I want to, all notions of what the next band over are doing, punk-rock, etc, it's all past, it's left my head. I want to feel natural with it now.

also by Lee Ranaldo
Road Movies
Bookstore
Moroccan Journal: Jajouka Excerpt (with Leah Singer)

to Credits

pictures: LR. **Back cover, lower picture:** Leah Singer. **Author photo:** Al Arthur,
he sessions for the first SY EP, 1982. *ii:* First night out: LR poster design for
ns Savage Blunder '82 Tour. *iii:* CBGB's ad, early '80s. **28-9:** "Blood on Brighton
First UK tour, 1985. **46:** "Blown Off." An English fan's cartoon, late '80s.
ac Ranch, Amarillo, Texas, by LR, 1987. **110-1:** Sonic Scotland, late '80s.
dreaming in a Daydream Nation, 1988, by Michael Lavine.

also from Soft Skull Press...

Soft Skull Press
98 Suffolk St. #3A • NYC • 10002

The Kentucky Rules

by Cynthia Nelson
with illustrations by Tara Jane O'Neil

Indie-rock sensations Cynthia Nelson and Tara Jane O'Neil
return to press with a second collaboration in poetry and art,
following their acclaimed Soft Skull collection *Raven Days*. With
their band Retsin and books like *The Kentucky Rules*, Cynthia
and Tara have created a body of work that supports an earthy,
direct, self-possessed vision.

the haiku year

by Tom Gilroy, Anna Grace, Jim McKay, Douglas A. Martin, Grant
Lee Phillips, Rick Roth, and Michael Stipe

"The beautifully designed *haiku year* consists of daily haiku written
by a group of seven friends....There are some pretty awesome haiku
here. Here's one: 'Before you could hang up/my machine caught/
a half-second of bar noise.'"

—*JANE* Magazine
August 1998

"The real revolution will begin when we all start communicating
with each other with love, honesty and purity of heart—and thi
book is a three-line leap in that direction
—Todd Co

Distributed to the trade by Consortium Book Sales & Distribution, 1-800-283-3
Access www.softskull.com for the latest Soft Skull catalog, text, and inform

."

by

572

ation.